Target 9
Get back on track

Pearson Edexcel GCSE (9–1)
History

Weimar and Nazi Germany, 1918–39

Rob Bircher

Pearson

Published by Pearson Education Limited, 80 Strand, London, WC2R ORL.

www.pearsonschoolsandfecolleges.co.uk

Copies of official specifications for all Pearson qualifications may be found on the website: qualifications.pearson.com

Text and illustrations © Pearson Education Ltd 2018
Typeset and illustrated by Newgen KnowledgeWorks Pvt. Ltd. Chennai, India
Produced by Out of House Publishing Solutions

The right of Rob Bircher to be identified as author of this work has been asserted by him in accordance with the Copyright, Designs and Patents Act 1988.

First published 2018

21 20 19 18
10 9 8 7 6 5 4 3 2 1

British Library Cataloguing in Publication Data
A catalogue record for this book is available from the British Library

ISBN 978 1 292 24522 5

Printed in Slovakia by Neografia

Acknowledgements
The authors and publisher would like to thank the following individuals and organisations for their kind permission to reproduce copyright material.

Text Credits
5 Stefan Zweig: Stefan Zweig, "A German citizen recalls what everyday life was like in Germany in 1923" **8 German Labour front:** Robert Ley, "A joke from 1930s Germany", the leader of the German Labour Front, is asking questions of the manager of a factory **9 SOPADE:** From a SOPADE report in 1934 **81 Joseph Goebbels:** Goebbels," From a speech to representatives of the press (newspaper and radio) on 15 March 1933 about the world of the Ministry for Popular Enlightenment" **21 Adolf Hitler:** From Hitler's response to being charged with treason at his trial following the Munich Putsch in February 1924 **25 E. S. Mittler & Sohn:** Lurker Otto, Hitler hinter Festungsmauern: ein Bild aus trüben Tagen, E. S. Mittler & Sohn, 1933 **27 German federal government:** A report on Hitler by the Bavarian police after Hitler applied for early release from Landsberg prison **81 Freikorps:** Freikorps, A letter written by a soldier to his family, April 1920 **81 Social Democratic Party of Germany:** A letter written to a Social Democratic Party newspaper in 1919 **31 International Labour Organization:** Data from International Labour Review for the years 1929–33, International Labour Organization **31 JA Cloake:** JA Cloake, Germany 1918–1945, OUP 1997, p. 37 **35 Taylor & Francis:** Lea Grundig, Gesichte und Geschichte, 10th edn, Reprinted by permission of Dietz verlag **81 Anonymous:** From a pamphlet written and distributed by a group of banned communists in April 1933. **81 Elisabeth Gebensleben:** From private letters written in March and April 1933 by Elisabeth Gebensleben, a 49-year-old Nazi supporter and wife of her town's deputy mayor, to her friend Irmgard Brester. **82 Hans-Joachim Marseille:** From a letter by 'Hans J.' sent to the Social Democratic Party headquarters in Hanover on 9 March 1933 **82 Library of congress:** From the diary of Victor Klemperer, a Jewish university lecturer living in Germany in 1933 **41 Hodder & Stoughton:** Evans David,Years of Weimar and the Third Reich, Hodder & Stoughton, 1999 **49 Nelson-Hall:** Morris warren Bayard, The Weimar Republic and Nazi Germany, Nelson-Hall, 1982 **46 Routledge:** Roderick Stackelberg, Hitler's Germany: Origins, Interpretations, Legacies, Routledge, 2002 **46 Harper & Row:** Alan Bullock, Hitler: a study in tyranny, Harper & Row, 1962 **82 Blandford Press:** John McKenzie, Weimar Germany: 1918–1933, Blandford Press, 1971 **82 Hodder Education:** Geoff Layton, From Second Reich to Third Reich--Germany, 1918–1945, Hodder Education, 2008 **82 Hodder & Stoughton:** David Evans, Years of Weimar and the Third Reich, Hodder & Stoughton, 1999 **83 Pearson Education:** John child, Edexcel GCSE (9–1) History Weimar and Nazi Germany, 1918–1939 Student Book, Pearson Education Limited, 2016 **58 Penguin Books:** The Third Reich in Power by Richard J. Evans (Author)P114, 2007 **58 Hachette UK:** John Wright, Steve Waugh, Hodder GCSE History for Edexcel: Weimar and Nazi Germany, 1918–39, Hachette UK, 2016 **61 Hodder Education Group:** David Evans, Jane Jenkins, Years of Wiemar the Third Reich and Post-War Germany, Hodder Education Group, 2008 **61 Routledge:** John Hiden, The Weimar Republic, Routledge, 2014 **69 Hachette UK:** David Ferriby, Dave Martin, AQA GCSE History: Understanding the Modern World, Hachette UK, 2016 **69 Alpha history:** Jennifer Llewellyn, Jim Southey and Steve Thompson, A modern history website, Alpha History, published in 2014 **71 Oxford University Press:** Richard Bessel, Life in the Third Reich, Oxford University Press, 1987 **71 Alpha history:** Jennifer Llewellyn, Jim Southey and Steve Thompson, A modern history website, Alpha History, published in 2014 **74 Düsseldorf:** From a report to the Gestapo by the Düsseldorf branch of the Nazi Party. This report was made in 1943 **79 Pearson education:** From Germany 1918–1945, by Steve Waugh, published in 2013 **79 Pearson Education:** From Germany 1918–1945, by Steve Waugh, published in 2013 **79 Penguin Books:** The Third Reich in Power by Richard J. Evans (Author)P268

Photographs (Key: b-bottom; c-centre; l-left; r-right; t-top)

Alamy Stock Photo: World History Archive 2, Chronicle 34, World History Archive 21,22. Fotolibra: Jackie Fox 6

Notes from the publisher
1. While the publishers have made every attempt to ensure that advice on the qualification and its assessment is accurate, the official specification and associated guidance materials are the only authoritative source of information and should always be referred to for definitive guidance. Pearson examiners have not contributed to any sections in this resource relevant to examination papers for which they have responsibility.
2. Pearson has robust editorial processes, including answer and fact checks, to ensure the accuracy of the content in this publication, and every effort is made to ensure this publication is free of errors. We are, however, only human, and occasionally errors do occur. Pearson is not liable for any misunderstandings that arise as a result of errors in this publication, but it is our priority to ensure that the content is accurate. If you spot an error, please do contact us at resourcescorrections@pearson.com so we can make sure it is corrected.

Contents

① Making inferences

This unit will help you to draw inferences from sources and support them when answering a question. The skills you will build are how to:

- make an inference from a source
- make inferences that are relevant to the question
- back up inferences with relevant detail.

This unit is about making inferences from a source (Source A on page 2). The unit will build your skills in tackling the source inference question efficiently.

Exam-style question

Give **two** things you can infer from Source A about financial problems in 1923.

Complete the table below to explain your answer.

i	What I can infer:
	....
	Details in the source that tell me this:
	....
ii	What I can infer:
	....
	Details in the source that tell me this:
	....

(4 marks)

Making inferences is about squeezing more information from a source than it actually tells you.

The three key questions in the **skills boosts** will help you to develop your skills to make inferences.

 1 How do I make a valid inference from a source?

2 How do I make inferences that are relevant to the question?

 3 How do I support my inferences with relevant detail?

The key to success with this question is to make **two** valid inferences from the source and support each of them with detail from the source.

Study Source A below and then answer the questions that follow it.

Source A | A photo from 1923, showing German children playing with bundles of banknotes.

(1) Which one of the following is a valid inference about Source A on this page? Tick ✓ your choice.

A	Children are playing with stacks of money and have made a tower out of the money.	☐
B	This photo is connected to hyperinflation because that was when people had to carry money around in wheelbarrows.	☐
C	The source is a photo, which makes it a reliable record of an actual event, but it could have been set up or staged, which would reduce its usefulness.	☐
D	In 1923 this huge amount of money probably was not very valuable because otherwise adults wouldn't have let children play with it like this.	✓

(2) Why were the other options in (1) **not** valid inferences? Next to each of the three explanations below, write ✎ the letter of the rejected option from (1) that it describes.

(a)	This statement is based on the student's own knowledge, not from the source itself. It is correct, but not a valid inference.	B
(b)	This is a statement about source usefulness, not an inference.	C
(c)	This is a description of what the source shows, not an inference about what the source implies.	A

Making inferences is a skill that needs practice. Learning to answer source inference questions efficiently will leave you more time to answer the higher-mark questions. You should aim to spend no more than 6 minutes on this exam-style question. We will do more work on making inferences in the first skills boost on page 5.

The early challenges to the Weimar Republic, 1919–23

This unit uses the theme of the early challenges to the Weimar Republic to build your skills in making inferences. If you need to review your knowledge of this theme, work through these pages.

(1) Tick ✓ the topics below that would count as early challenges to the Weimar Republic (1919–23), and put a cross ✗ by those that would not (e.g. because they come from later than 1923).

A	'Stab in the back' theory	☐
B	The Locarno Pact	☒
C	The Kapp Putsch	☑
D	The Spartacist Revolt	☑
E	The Treaty of Versailles	☐
F	The Bamberg Conference	☒

(2) Draw 🖉 lines linking these terms from the Treaty of Versailles (1919) with the correct facts and figures.

A Reparations were fixed at	a 15 years
B The German army was limited to	b 11
C A million Germans became Polish citizens with the loss of	c 136,000 million marks
D Allied troops were stationed in the demilitarised Rhineland until	d 1930
E Output from the Saar coalfields went to France for	e 100,000 men
F The number of German colonies made mandates for victorious countries	f Posen and West Prussia

(3) For each of the following ideas, write 🖉 a sentence explaining how it weakened the Weimar Republic.

a The 'November Criminals'

....

....

b The 'Diktat'

....

....

④ After the elections of 6 June 1920, the three main moderate parties that supported the Weimar Republic won only 45% of the seats in the new Reichstag. But which parties were which? Fill in the empty cells in the table below.

Extremist left wing		Moderate parties				Extremist right wing
		DDP	ZP	DVP	DNVP	NSDAP
Communist Party	Social Democrats	Democrats		People's Party	National Party	Nazi Party
Opposed Weimar Republic	Supported Weimar Republic			Sometimes supported Republic	Grudgingly accepted Republic	

⑤ Which three of the events below go together to produce an effective summary of the events of the Spartacist Revolt? Number your choices 1, 2 and 3 to show the order they should go in.

A Ebert's government was struggling to control the Freikorps. The threat of being disbanded sparked an uprising against the government. ☐

B The Freikorps were armed and were able to clear the rioting workers off the streets. Luxemburg and Liebknecht were arrested and killed. ☐

C Thousands of workers took to the streets to protest after Ebert sacked the police chief of Berlin. The Spartacists saw this as a chance to organise an uprising against the government. ☐

D Ebert, the chancellor of the Weimar Republic, told the Reichswehr, 'No enemy defeated you'. ☐

E Ebert ordered Reichswehr officers to organise demobilised soldiers into Freikorps units. Some 250,000 Freikorps were turned on the rioting workers. ☐

⑥ Tick ✓ 'true' or 'false' after each of the following statements about the Kapp Putsch.

		true	false
a	General Seeckt, head of the Reichswehr, helped Ebert to resist the Freikorps rebels' march on Berlin.	☐	☐
b	Wolfgang Kapp seized control of Berlin and made himself leader of the German republic.	☐	☐
c	The rebels invited the Kaiser to come back from exile and rule Germany again.	☐	☐
d	Members of the Weimar government fled Berlin. They could not put the revolt down by force.	☐	☐
e	Weimar ministers urged people not to co-operate with the rebel government, but this failed because the people wanted the Kaiser to return.	☐	☐

How do I make a valid inference from a source?

A valid inference is one that is directly supported by the source content. There are three common problems to avoid.

- An inference is something the source implies – an underlying message. You should not write a description of what it says or shows.
- A valid inference has to come from the source, not be based on what else you know about the topic.
- Answering inference questions is about keeping it simple, not writing more than you need to or taking more time than you need: these are 4-mark questions.

Study the source below, then answer the questions that follow it.

Exam-style question

Give **two** things you can infer from Source A about the challenges of 1923 for the Weimar Republic.

Source A   *A German citizen, Stefan Zweig, recalls what everyday life was like in Germany in 1923.*

On streetcars one paid in millions, trucks carried the paper money from the Reichsbank to the other banks, and a fortnight later one found hundred thousand mark notes in the gutter; a beggar had thrown them away contemptuously. A pair of shoelaces cost more than a shoe had once cost; no, more than a fashionable shoe store with two thousand pairs of shoes had cost before; to repair a broken window cost more than the whole house had formerly cost…

The unemployed stood around by the thousands and shook their fists at the profiteers and foreigners in their luxurious cars who bought whole rows of streets like a box of matches.

(1) Students were asked to make a valid inference from Source A, above. Read the three student answers below and tick ✓ the one that has done the best job of avoiding the three obstacles listed at the top of this page.

A | *Printing money to pay loans and reparation payments had caused hyperinflation.* | ☐

B | *Source A is describing the situation in 1923 when Germany was hit by hyperinflation. It suggests that prices for everyday objects had now reached unbelievably, ridiculously high levels and that the situation was causing social tension, e.g. between the poor and those rich people who had been able to make money from the situation.* | ☐

C | *The situation in 1923 was causing tension between unemployed people and people who had been able to make money out of the situation, including foreigners.* | ☐

(2) Using the list at the top of this page, annotate ✏ the two answers you did not select with feedback to show how they could be improved.

2 How do I make inferences that are relevant to the question?

You may be able to infer many different things from a source, so one important skill to develop is the ability to make appropriate inferences that are **relevant to the question**.

Exam-style question

Give **two** things you can infer from Source A below about reactions in Germany to the terms of the Treaty of Versailles.

Source A *A cartoon published in July 1919 in a German newspaper. The figure of the girl on the bed represents Germany. The vampire figure represents Georges Clemenceau, the French prime minister.*

① Which of the following pieces of advice is correct? Tick ✓ your choice.

A | A valid inference is based on your historical knowledge about the topic. | ☐

B | A valid inference starts by describing what you can see in the source. | ☐

C | A valid inference is directly supported by the content of the source. | ☐

② Read the following student answer and annotate 🖉 it to show where this student has gone wrong.

> The cartoon is about reparations, which was money Germany paid to other countries (including France) for the damage done by the First World War.

Cartoons are challenging sources to work with because the meanings are hidden. Read the source information very carefully for the key information that will help to unlock the meanings.

③ **a** Which one of these inferences is both valid (directly supported from the source) and relevant to the question? Tick ✓ your choice.

A | France was seen as an enemy. | ☐

B | German people were frightened of the French because they might attack them. | ☐

C | The French prime minister was seen as 'sucking the life' out of Germany. | ☐

D | The French prime minister was blamed for the harshness of the Treaty to Germany. | ☐

b Write 🖉 a brief explanation of your answer to ③ **a**.

....

....

....

....

How do I support my inferences with relevant detail?

For success with this type of exam-style question, your two inferences need to be backed up with supporting detail taken from the source.

1 Look back at Source A on page 5 and the exam-style question that went with it. Find detail in that source to support the following two inferences made by a student. Write ✏ your supporting detail in the space provided.

Plan to write four sentences for this type of exam-style question:
- inference 1 + detail to support it
- inference 2 + detail to support it.

a What I can infer: *People who had lost their jobs blamed people who had profited from hyperinflation.*	Details in the source that tell me this:
b What I can infer: *Some people were able to benefit from hyperinflation.*	Details in the source that tell me this:

2 Now do the same for these two inferences from Source A on page 6. ✏

a What I can infer: *The Treaty was seen as weakening Germany too much.*	Details in the source that tell me this:
b What I can infer: *The French were blamed for deliberately weakening Germany.*	Details in the source that tell me this:

For efficient supporting detail, select only what you need to do the job. This could be a precise quote from the source, a concise paraphrase of something the source says, or a brief description of what a visual source shows.

3 This student has written a good answer for the exam-style question on page 1, but they have written too much. Revise the answer by crossing out ~~cat~~ unnecessary text so the answer makes the same points in four brief sentences.

> *Because of the hyperinflation, everyday life became very difficult for most people because money stopped having any real value in 1923: people needed millions of marks just to pay for really ordinary things. Source A shows this with bundles of banknotes in the photo being used as toys by children, which would never usually have happened because money used to be really valuable and if the children had lost even one banknote or damaged even one banknote it would have been a waste.*
>
> *Hyperinflation also meant there were very large numbers of banknotes in circulation, which meant people had to find ways of transporting all the cash they needed, making life difficult especially since the money had to be spent quickly before it lost its value. Source A shows this because it suggests that the one family represented by the children in the photo had got so much money that the children have enough to make a large pyramid out of it, with bundles of banknotes to spare.*

Sample response

Now you have refined your inference skills, you can answer the inference question in the exam efficiently, helping you save time that you can spend on higher-mark questions.

Read the following exam-style question and Source A, and the student answer that follows.

Exam-style question

Give **two** things you can infer from Source A about support for the Nazi regime among Germans.

Source A *A joke from 1930s Germany. Robert Ley, the leader of the German Labour Front, is asking questions of the manager of a factory.*

Ley: Tell me, have you got any Social Democrats with you?

Manager: Oh yes, about half the workforce.

Ley: How dreadful! But surely no Communists?

Manager: Oh yes, about a third of the men.

Ley: Really! What about Democrats and so on?

Manager: They make up the remaining 20 per cent.

Ley: Good gracious! Haven't you got any Nazis at all?

Manager: Oh yes, of course, all of them are Nazis!

Exam-style question

i   What I can infer:

The source suggests that the Nazis were worried about whether many ordinary people supported them. Details in the source that tell me this:

This is shown in Source A by the questions Robert Ley, the leader of the German Labour Front asks, such as 'Haven't you got any Nazis at all?'.

ii   What I can infer:

Some Germans said they supported the Nazis even if they actually had different political views. Details in the source that tell me this:

This is shown in Source A by the joke punchline, which says that although no one believes in Nazi politics, 'of course, all of them are Nazis'.

(4 marks)

(1) Complete the following checklist for this answer by ticking ✓ the columns in the table.

Checklist How well does the answer...	Not done ✓	Did one but not both ✓	Did both ✓
identify two valid inferences from the source?			
make sure each inference relates to the question?			
back up both inferences with detail from the source?			

(2) How could the student make their answer more concise? Cross out ~~cat~~ any unnecessary words in the responses above.

(3) The student spent 10 minutes writing this answer and is hoping to get a level 9 in History. What feedback would you give them to help them achieve their goal? Write ✐ your answer here.

....

....

Your turn!

(1) Put your skills to the test with this exam-style question on the topic of changes in living standards for German workers under the Nazi regime. ✎

Exam-style question

Give **two** things you can infer from Source A about changes in living standards for German workers under the Nazis.

Complete the table below to explain your answer.

i	What I can infer:
	....
	....
	....
	Details in the source that tell me this:
	....
	....
	....
ii	What I can infer:
	....
	....
	....
	Details in the source that tell me this:
	....
	....
	....

(4 marks)

Source A *From a SOPADE report in 1934. SOPADE was the organisation of SPD members in exile in Prague from 1933 to 1938. It received reports about life under the Nazis through a secret correspondence system.*

Southern Bavaria:

The *'Kraft durch Freude'* trips are really popular here. The numerous visits which the mountain villages get from them is stimulating our tourist trade considerably. … A few days ago I met a married couple from Cologne. For an 8-day stay in Frasdorf, including the journey there and back, costs and apartment, two people had paid 60 Marks. Otherwise the journey alone… would have cost 100 Marks. … In any case, thanks to *'Kraft durch Freude'*, a lot of people from simple backgrounds are now enjoying lovely holiday trips. This success is making a good impression. But the Nazis also use it well for their propaganda.

Kraft durch Freude: Strength through Joy

Remember: make sure your two inferences are valid (relevant to the question focus) and that they are inferences, not descriptions. You may find writing 'Source A suggests…' is a good way to make sure you infer rather than describe.

Back up each inference with precisely selected detail. Select a phrase from the source (only what's needed!), or concisely paraphrase a source detail, or briefly describe an element of a visual source.

Review your skills

Check up

Review your response to the exam-style question on page 9. Tick ✓ the column to show how well you think you have done each of the following.

Had a go ✓   **Nearly there** ✓   **Got it!** ✓

identified two valid inferences

made sure each inference relates to the question

supported the inferences with details from the source

used concise language to answer efficiently

Look over all of your work in this unit. Note down ✎ on a separate piece of paper the three most important things to remember about how best to make inferences.

Need more practice?

If you want to practise another exam-style question, study Source A on page 81 and then answer ✎ the question below. Continue on a separate piece of paper if necessary.

Exam-style question

Give **two** things you can infer from Source A about the role of Goebbels as Minister for Propaganda.

i   What I can infer:

....

....

Details in the source that tell me this:

....

....

ii   What I can infer:

....

....

Details in the source that tell me this:

....

....

(4 marks)

How confident do you feel about each of these **skills**? Colour in ✎ the bars.

1 How do I make a valid inference from a source?

2 How do I make inferences that are relevant to the question?

3 How do I support my inferences with relevant detail?

② Explaining causes

This unit focuses on the skills needed for explaining causes. The skills you will build are how to:

- analyse the topic to identify causes
- make sure explanations link to the question focus
- support explanations with your own knowledge.

Exam-style question

Explain why there was an economic recovery in the Weimar Republic in the years 1924–29.

You may use the following in your answer:

- the Rentenmark
- reparation payments

You **must** also use information of your own.

(12 marks)

The economic recovery of the Weimar Republic is quite a wide area of content. The two bullet points in this question, called stimulus points, suggest two aspects of this content that you could use in your answer. To write a good answer to a question like this, you should aim to address **three** aspects of this content. It is up to you which three aspects you choose.

You then need to use explanation to show how the aspects you have chosen **caused** the event or change mentioned in the exam-style question – in this case, why there was economic recovery in the Weimar Republic in the years 1924–29. What you are doing is turning the aspects into causes by linking them back to the question.

1918-1923 = NEW WEIMAR REPUBLIC - UPRISINGS
                                  - TOV
                                  - HYPERINFLATION...

1924-1929 = GOLDEN YEARS- STRESEMANN FIXING GERMANY.
         HAVE MONEY. - LOCARNO PACT
                     - LEAGUE OF NATIONS.

1929-1933 = RIZE OF THE NAZIS - WALL STREET
                              - G DEPRESSION
                              - SA
                              - VON PAPEN...

1933-1939= NAZI GERMANY.

The three key questions in the **skills boosts** will help you to develop your understanding of the skills involved in explaining causes.

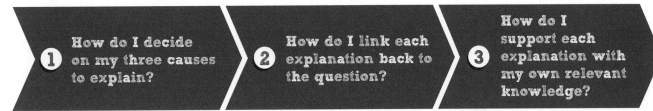

① How do I decide on my three causes to explain?

② How do I link each explanation back to the question?

③ How do I support each explanation with my own relevant knowledge?

Here is a student's plan to answer the exam-style question on page 11.

Intro	Stresemann was successful in stabilising Germany's economy	
	Points	**Supporting information**
Cause 1	The stabilisation of the currency was an important cause of economic recovery because it ended hyperinflation	
	• Rentenmark → in 1924 it stabilised the economy	• Set up in 1923 (by Stresemann)
	• Then Reichsmark was backed by gold reserves	• 1 Rentenmark = 1 million million old marks
	• How it ended hyperinflation	
Cause 2	The Dawes Plan was an important cause because of reduction in reparation payments	
	• Dawes Plan – reduced reparation payment and US loans	• Dawes Plan – 1924
	• Reparations crisis ended; German industry recovered	• Reduced reparations to £50 million p.a.
	• Confidence increased	• US loans were $25 billion, 1924–30
		• German industrial output doubled in 1923–28
Cause 3	Young Plan was an important cause because it allowed tax reductions	
	• Young Plan – reparations reduced more	• Young Plan – 1929
	• Important because reduced tax meant political stability	• £6.6 billion
		• French agreed to leave Ruhr in 1930
		• 1929 referendum: 85% support for Young Plan

1. You need to cover three aspects of content (areas of the topic) in total – these can include one or both of the exam-style question's stimulus points, or they can be all your own. Circle (A) text to indicate where the student has used any of the exam-style question's stimulus points in their plan.

2. The exam-style question says 'you **must** also use information of your own'. Underline (A) where the student has planned to use their own information in their answer.

3. What do you think the strengths of this plan are? Tick ✓ the things you think it does well.

   A | The answer includes three causes. | ✓

   B | The student uses their own knowledge in their answer. | ✓

   C | Each cause answers the question focus. | ✓

   D | Each cause is supported by the student's own knowledge. | ✓

4. Now write ✐ a brief evaluation of the plan's strengths and weaknesses.

....

....

....

....

The recovery of the Republic and changes in society, 1924–29

This unit uses the theme of the recovery of the Republic and changes in society 1924–29 to build your skills in explaining causes. If you need to review your knowledge of this theme, work through these pages.

1. Different reasons for the recovery of the Weimar Republic in the period 1924–29 are listed below, together with information to support them. Draw ✏ lines linking each reason to the correct supporting information.

Reasons for recovery	Supporting information
A Gustav Stresemann ended resistance in the Ruhr and negotiated the Dawes Plan.	**a** Germany regained full control over its most important industrial area.
B The Rentenmark stabilised the currency and helped to restore confidence in the economy.	**b** The $200 billion was mainly funded by bonds issued from Wall Street.
C The Dawes Plan restructured reparations and solved the crisis over the Ruhr.	**c** Germany had no gold reserves left in 1923, so it was backed by the mortgaged value of land.
D US loans to German industry helped industry to recover and also funded reparation payments.	**d** Reparations were split into two components: a part that had to be paid, and the rest which was only paid if it would not damage Germany.
E The Young Plan aimed to continue the support of the Weimar government by further reducing reparation payments.	**e** Leader of the German People's Party, Chancellor in 1923, foreign secretary to 1929.

2. Complete ✏ this table explaining Stresemann's foreign policy achievements. Fill in the missing information in the middle column, then add both positive and negative impacts on Germany in the final column. Continue on a separate piece of paper if necessary.

Policy	What the policy did	Impact on Germany
The Locarno Pact (1925)	A treaty between Germany, Britain, France, Italy and Belgium that DEMILITARISED THE RHINELAND + FIXED THE BORDERS	GIVEN A VOICE.
Joining the League of Nations (1926)	Germany was accepted into the LEAGUE OF NATIONS.	THEY'D BE INVOLVED WITH FOREIGN COMMUNICATIONS.
The Kellogg-Briand Pact (1928)	A pact in 1928 between 15 countries plus Germany, later signed by over 60 nations, that WAR WOULD NOT BE USED TO GAIN POWER.	ESTABLISHED AS AN EQUAL WITH OTHER POWERFUL COUNTRIES.

3 Use the statements below to fill in ✐ the gaps in the following text about changes for women in the Weimar Republic.

Two reasons why women got the right to vote in Germany after the war were popular support for ......(5)......, and the belief of the Social Democrats, ...(7)......, that women should have the vote. As a result, women won the right to vote and the right to stand for elections in November 1918. This had important consequences for Weimar elections: 90% of women voters turned out for Weimar elections and by 1932, ...(6)...... .

Article 109 ......(1)......, including equal rights at work and in marriage. However, women were not always treated fairly. Two examples of this are that ......(4)...... in jobs where men and women did the same work, and women were expected to leave their jobs when they got married. Although 75% of women had jobs during the war, but ......(8)...... .

Some women, especially young unmarried women working in city jobs, rejected traditional roles for women. ......(3)...... through fashion and behaviour: for example, ...(2)......, and revealing clothes, and smoking and drinking, ...(9)...... .

of the Weimar Constitution guaranteed important rights for women (1)	women were paid around one-third less than men (4)	who led the Weimar government in 1918 (7)
short haircuts, more make-up (2)	the way women had worked for the war effort (5)	this figure had halved by 1925 (8)
These 'new women' expressed their independence (3)	10% of Reichstag members were women (6)	and going out unaccompanied by men (9)

4 The sentences below are about changes in society 1924–29. Tick ✓ the sentences you think are correct.

A	Between 1924 and 1931 more than 2 million new homes were built, reducing homelessness in Germany by 60%.	✓
B	Between 1924 and 1931 more than 6 million new homes were built, reducing homelessness in Germany by 20%.	
C	Unemployment in 1928 had fallen by 700,000: from 2 million in 1926 to 1.3 million in 1928.	✓
D	Unemployment in 1928 had fallen by 4.5 million: from 4.8 million in 1926 to 0.3 million in 1928.	

How do I decide on my three causes to explain?

Your answer should aim to explain three causes. You need to be able to do two things well with each cause:
- **explain** securely how it caused the question focus
- **support** it with your own knowledge.

You can use your own knowledge instead of the stimulus points, but you must still cover three aspects of content, including a range of information for each.

Page 12 showed one approach to planning your answer using the exam-style question on page 11. If you are not sure which causes to explain, you might find it best to start with a spider diagram to **analyse** possible causes of the question focus.

1 a Complete the following tasks on a separate piece of paper.

   i   Write the question focus in the middle and around it quickly write all the causes you remember.

   ii For each cause, write an **explanation**: *because…*

   iii For each cause, add evidence from your own knowledge to **support** your explanation:
       this is shown by… or Back up:

   iv See how many causes you can add explanations and evidence to.

b Tick ✓ your best three. These do not have to include the question stimulus points if you are more confident about answering for other causes.

> Events in history usually have multiple causes. Analysis means breaking something down into the parts that make it up. You are using analysis skills when you break down the different aspects of a topic area and explain each of them in turn.

Here is an example of a student's 'analysis diagram' for the same exam-style question.

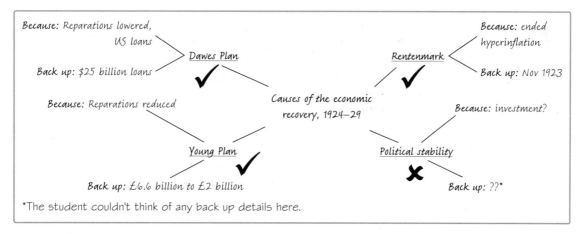

Because: Reparations lowered, US loans
Back up: $25 billion loans
Dawes Plan ✓

Because: Reparations reduced
Young Plan ✓
Back up: £6.6 billion to £2 billion

Causes of the economic recovery, 1924–29

Because: ended hyperinflation
Rentenmark ✓
Back up: Nov 1923

Because: investment?
Political stability ✗
Back up: ??*

*The student couldn't think of any back up details here.

2 Now draw your own 'analysis diagram' for the following exam-style question on a separate piece of paper.

Exam-style question

Explain why Stresemann's foreign policies helped the Weimar Republic's recovery.

You may use the following in your answer:
- the League of Nations
- the Kellogg-Briand Pact

You **must** also use information of your own.

(12 marks)

2 How do I link each explanation back to the question?

Each of your three explanations must link back to the question.

Consider this exam-style question.

Exam-style question

Explain why the position of women in German society improved under the Weimar Republic.

You may use the following in your answer:

- votes for women (November 1918)
- women in the workplace

You **must** also use information of your own.

(12 marks)

Let's assume that your third change of this topic is Article 109 of the Weimar Constitution. A good way of making sure your answer stays locked on to the question focus is to start each explanation like this:

[(Cause)] + [question focus] + because...

For example:

(Votes for women) improved the position of women in German society because

(1) Try this out for yourself with the exam-style question on page 11. Use the annotation system from above.

THE RENTENMARK HELPED BRING ECONOMIC RECOVERY IN THE WEIMAR REPUBLIC BECAUSE

(2) Now use this approach to complete these three explanations for the question above.

Cause	Explanation	Supporting information
Votes for women (November 1918)	This improved the position of women in German society because THEY COULD NOW VOTE AS WELL AS MEN	90% of women voters used their vote, so politicians were keener to promote policies benefiting women
Women in the workplace	This improved the position of women in German society because THEY COULD HAVE JOBS, RATHER THAN JUST STAYING AT HOME.	Retail and services boomed, which meant many more jobs for women: more money and freedom
The Weimar Constitution (Article 109)	This improved the position of women in German society because THEY WERE NOW SEEN AS EQUAL TO MEN.	Equal rights for women: women should be able to enter all professions on an equal basis with men

3 How do I support each explanation with my own relevant knowledge?

Each of your explanations needs to be backed up by accurate supporting information. Your supporting information needs to be just as relevant to the question as your explanations are.

Study this exam-style question then answer the questions that follow it.

Exam-style question

Explain why standards of living improved in Germany between 1923 and 1929.

You may use the following in your answer:

- Unemployment Insurance Act (1927)
- building new houses

You **must** also use information of your own.

(12 marks)

Here is a student's plan for an answer to this question. Each explanation must include at least one piece of accurate and relevant information that directly supports it.

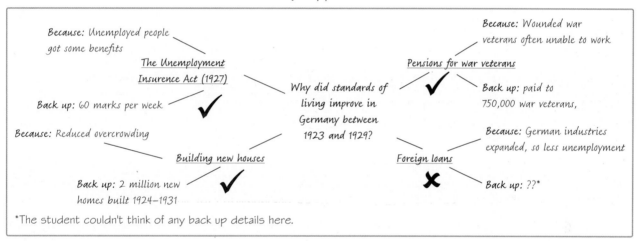

*The student couldn't think of any back up details here.

The following extract from the student's answer to the question uses this supporting information. It also shows how the information is relevant to the question by making links to the question focus.

① ⓐ Underline Ⓐ where the student has used supporting information.

ⓑ Circle Ⓐ where the student has made links to the question to show how the supporting information is relevant.

> The Unemployment Insurance Act (1927) helped standards of living improve between 1923 and 1929 because it provided unemployment and sickness benefit to German workers. In 1924, over 4% of the total workforce was unemployed. The Unemployment Insurance Act charged 16.4 million workers 3% of their wages: this money was used to provide an average of 60 marks per week in benefits for those out of work or unable to work, which substantially improved standards of living for those receiving the payments.

② On a separate piece of paper, complete ✏ this student's answer by explaining another two reasons why standards of living improved. Use the plan to help you. Back up both explanations with accurate supporting information, and remember to make links to the question focus to show how it is relevant.

Sample response

In this unit you have practised skills for explaining causes and ensuring that your argument remains focused on the question. Have a go at assessing and improving the following student answer to this exam-style question.

Exam-style question

Explain why tensions in German society increased in the years 1924 to 1929.

You may use the following in your answer:

- 'new women'
- cultural changes

You **must** also use information of your own.

(12 marks)

Even though there were significant improvements for people living under the Weimar Republic, there were also many tensions in German society. 'New women' caused tensions because they deliberately went against the traditional roles of women. They worked and were financially independent. They wore make-up and had short hair, which were not traditional. They also smoked and drank, and this was not accepted behaviour. Cultural changes like the paintings of Otto Dix, the Bauhaus school of design and Fritz Lang's films saw artists of all kinds trying out new ideas. Experimental work often criticised low standards of living or the horrors of the war. At the same time, many artists were supported by the Weimar government, which was criticised. Women's improving position in German society also caused social tensions between 1924 and 1929 because many Germans objected to women taking on jobs while men were unemployed. Despite economic recovery under Stresemann, unemployment never dipped below 1.3 million in Weimar Germany and many jobs were not very secure. The Weimar constitution (Article 109) gave women equal rights in the workplace and in the marriage partnership. German conservatives strongly objected to this and resisted paying women equal wages or letting women into certain professions. By 1925, only 36% of women were in work, the same as before the war, because of pressures on women to stay at home or to only work in certain professions, for example shop work rather than high-status jobs like lawyers. So the Weimar government's aim of equality for women met strong opposition and this increased social tensions.

---

(1) Underline (A) places in the answer where the student has used detail to support the points made in their answer. Annotate (✏) the answer with these details.

(2) Circle (A) where the student could have done more to link their answer to the question. Annotate (✏) the answer with suggestions of how this could be improved.

(3) Evaluate the strengths and weaknesses of this answer by ticking (✓) the relevant points in this checklist.

(4) Now write (✏) a brief piece of advice for the student on a separate piece of paper to show how they can improve this answer.

Checklist	✓
The answer has three explanations.	✓
These explanations include the student's own knowledge.	✓
Each explanation is securely linked to the question focus.	
Each explanation is supported by relevant details from the student's own knowledge.	

Your turn!

To practise these skills, you are now going to write your own improved answer to this question from the previous page.

> **Exam-style question**
>
> Explain why tensions in German society increased in the years 1924 to 1929.
>
> You may use the following in your answer:
>
> • 'new women'
>
> • cultural changes
>
> You **must** also use information of your own.
>
> (12 marks)

① First, plan your answer by completing ✎ the table below.

Introduction	FROM THE YEARS 1924 TO 1929, TENSIONS IN GERMAN SOCIETY INCREASED.	
	Points	**Supporting information**
Link to question	WOMEN WERE TAKING ADVANTAGE OF FREEDOM, MANY MEN + OTHER WOMEN DISAGREED - THEY NEEDED WOMEN TO BE MOTHERS.	
Cause 1	NEW WOMEN	BIRTH RATE FALLING 1913 - 128 PER YEAR, 1925 - 80
Link to question	LEFT WING (KPD) COMMUNISTS. MONEY WAS BEING SPENT ON THIS, RATHER THAN ON WORKING PEOPLE. RIGHT WING (NAZI) SAID IT WAS AGAINST TRADITIONAL GERMAN CULTURE	
Cause 2	CULTURAL CHANGES	PAINTINGS OF OTTO DIX ARCHITECTS, ERICH MENDELSOHN, NEVER SEEN BEFORE.
Link to question	MANY INDUSTRIES WERE MALE DOMINATED, DIDN'T LIKE WOMEN W/ EQUAL PAY, OR THAT WOMEN WERE TAKING JOBS WHILST MEN WERE UNEMPLOYED.	
Cause 3	WOMENS EQUALITY.	ARTICLE 109 - EQUAL W/ MEN. VOTES - BY 1932 IC% REICHSTAG MEMBERS WERE FEMALE

② Now write ✎ your answer on a separate piece of paper. Remember:

• you should aim to provide explanations of three causes

• you can use the two stimulus points plus an aspect of content from your own knowledge, or one stimulus point plus two from your own knowledge, or all aspects from your own knowledge, but you must cover three aspects of content in total

• you should make sure each of the three causes explains how it caused the question focus

• you should make sure each of the three causes is supported with your own knowledge, and that this supporting information is just as relevant to the question as your explanation.

Review your skills

Check up

Review your response to the exam-style question on page 19. Tick ✓ the column to show how well you think you have done each of the following.

	Had a go ✓	Nearly there ✓	Got it! ✓
explained three causes	☐	☐	☐
securely linked each explanation to the question focus	☐	☐	☐
backed up each explanation with accurate and relevant supporting information	☐	☐	☐

Look over all of your work in this unit. Note down ✏ the three most important things to remember about how best to explain causes.

① ....

② ....

③ ....

Need more practice?

If you want to practise another exam-style question, try ✏ the one below, using your enhanced skills.

Exam-style question

Explain the causes of the Munich Putsch (1923).

You may use the following in your answer:

• the Treaty of Versailles

• hyperinflation

You **must** also use information of your own.

(12 marks)

How confident do you feel about each of these **skills**? Colour in ✏ the bars.

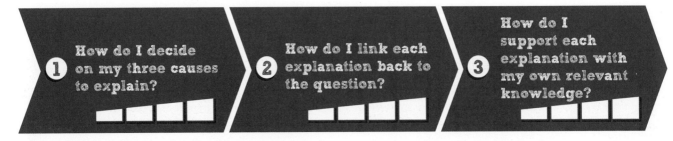

① How do I decide on my three causes to explain?

② How do I link each explanation back to the question?

③ How do I support each explanation with my own relevant knowledge?

③ Evaluating sources using provenance

This unit will help you to evaluate sources to determine their usefulness for a specific enquiry. The skills you will build are how to:

- analyse a source to select useful content
- use the nature and origin of the source to evaluate usefulness
- use the purpose of the source to evaluate usefulness.

The evaluation of source usefulness question is worth 8 marks and works like this.

Exam-style question

How useful are Sources B and C for an enquiry into reactions to Hitler's trial in 1924?

Source B *From Hitler's response to being charged with treason at his trial following the Munich Putsch in February 1924.*

I cannot declare myself guilty. True, I confess to the deed but I do not confess to the crime of high treason. There is no question of treason in an action which aims to undo the betrayal of this country in 1918. Besides, by no definition of treason can the deed of 8th and 9th November be called treason… And if we were committing treason, I am surprised that those who, at that time, had the same aims as I, are not standing beside me now… There is no such thing as high treason against the traitors of 1918.

Source C *A photo taken in February 1924 showing the defendants (those on trial) in the Munich Putsch Trial. Ludendorff and Hitler are standing side by side. Those wearing military dress are holding swords, which shows they are officers.*

The three key questions in the **skills boosts** will help you to analyse and evaluate source utility.

① How do I analyse a source to select potentially useful content?

② How can I use nature and origin to evaluate usefulness?

③ How can I use purpose to evaluate usefulness?

Provenance is the nature, origin and purpose (NOP) of the source. To recap:

This tells us the **nature** of the source: what type of source it is. In this case it is a statement recorded as part of a court trial. That affects this source's usefulness. Other types of sources, for example a diary entry or eyewitness account, would have different natures that would affect their usefulness in different ways.

This tells us the **origin** of the source: who wrote it or made it. In this case it is Adolf Hitler. That will be useful for understanding what people were reacting to. It limits usefulness in some ways, too: for example, it makes the source subjective rather than objective.

Source B — *From Hitler's response to being charged with treason at his trial following the Munich Putsch in February 1924.*

> I cannot declare myself guilty. True, I confess to the deed but I do not confess to the crime of high treason. There is no question of treason in an action which aims to undo the betrayal of this country in 1918. Besides, by no definition of treason can the deed of 8th and 9th November be called treason… And if we were committing treason, I am surprised that those who, at that time, had the same aims as I, are not standing beside me now… There is no such thing as high treason against the traitors of 1918.

The **purpose** of the source is about the reason it was written or made. Comparing the purpose of a source with what you know about the event being described can be a good way of judging source utility. How does Hitler's account of the Munich Putsch tally with what you know about his actions and statements during the Putsch?

In the exam, the two sources will appear in a Sources/Interpretation Booklet that is separate from the exam paper. The sources might be two texts, two images, or one of each.

(1) Here is the second source from page 21. In the source information below, circle (A) and label (✐) the nature, origin and purpose of the source.

Source C — *A photo taken in February 1924 showing the defendants (those on trial) in the Munich Putsch Trial. Ludendorff and Hitler are standing side by side. Those wearing military dress are holding swords, which shows they are officers.*

The Munich Putsch and its consequences

This unit uses the theme of the Munich Putsch to build your skills in analysing sources for usefulness. If you need to review your knowledge of this theme, work through these pages.

1 Categorise these causes of the Munich Putsch into short-, medium- and long-term causes in the table below.

| A Influence of Mussolini's Fascist Party, including March on Rome (1922) | B Growing social divisions | C Resentment against the Weimar Republic | D Rise in popularity of NSDAP: from 5,000 in 1922 to over 50,000 in 1923 |

| E Hyperinflation peaks (1923) | F The 'stab in the back' theory | G French occupation of the Ruhr (January 1923) | H The loss of Germany's colonies |

| I 'War guilt' and reparations | J Stresemann calling off the general strike in the Ruhr (September 1923) |

Short-term causes: current	Medium-term causes: recent	Long-term causes: historic

2 Draw lines to match the names of people involved in the Munich Putsch with their biographical details.

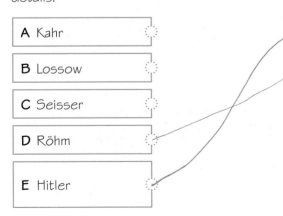

A Kahr		a Führer of the NSDAP
B Lossow		b co-founder and commander of the Sturmabteilung
C Seisser		c head of the Bavarian police
D Röhm		d head of the German army in Bavaria
E Hitler		e leader of the state government of Bavaria (State Commissioner)

3 Read the following statements describing the consequences of the Munich Putsch.

a Which statements are true and which are false? Tick ✓ the box next to each statement.

b Rewrite 🖉 the false statements to make them true. There is space below the list for this.

		true	false
A	Hitler and Ludendorff were charged with treason and put on trial, along with six others.	☐	☐
B	The trial was held in November 1923.	☐	☐
C	The trial did not receive much public attention.	☐	✓
D	Hitler was forbidden from speaking for himself in court because the judges thought his words might threaten law and order in Germany.	☐	✓
E	Hitler argued that if he was accused of treason then it was not fair that Kahr, Lossow and Seisser were not on trial for treason too, since they had also planned to overthrow the government.	☐	☐
F	Hitler and three others were found guilty and sentenced to five years' imprisonment. Röhm was put on probation. Ludendorff was acquitted.	✓	☐
G	Most Germans agreed with the sentences given to the Munich Putsch leaders.	☐	☐

....

....

....

....

....

....

....

4 Below are three longer-term consequences of the Munich Putsch. Write 🖉 a sentence on each, explaining how it went on to benefit Hitler and the Nazi Party.

a Hitler used his time in prison to write *Mein Kampf.*

....

....

b Hitler used the trial to set out his political views.

....

....

c Hitler decided that the strategy to take power by force would never succeed.

....

....

As well as understanding the causes, events and consequences of the Munich Putsch, considering different interpretations of the Putsch will also be useful. For example, was the Munich Putsch a failure, or was it a success?

How do I analyse a source to select potentially useful content?

The first task in answering this question is to analyse each source for useful content. This means picking out content that is potentially useful for a specific enquiry.

Exam-style question

How useful are Sources B and C for an enquiry into Hitler's change of approach for the Nazi Party after the Munich Putsch?

Source B — *From a book written by Otto Lurker called* Hitler Behind Prison Bars, *published in 1933. Lurker was a warder at Landsberg prison when Hitler was imprisoned there in 1924. Lurker later joined the SS.*

Hitler has shown himself to be an orderly, disciplined prisoner… He makes no exceptional demands, is calm and sensible, serious, in no way aggressive. … He is without personal vanity, is content with the prison diet, neither smokes nor drinks. … Hitler will undoubtedly try to revive enthusiasm for the National Movement as he sees it; he will not, however, employ his previous violent methods. … I have no hesitation in saying that Hitler's general behaviour under detention merits the grant of a probationary period.

① One piece of content from Source B is shown in the table below. Choose two more and add them to the table.

	✓
Hitler was an orderly, disciplined prisoner and not aggressive	

② Tick ✓ one piece of content above that is related directly to the enquiry in the question. Then make a statement to link it to how it helps the enquiry. For example, knowing that Hitler was not at all aggressive in prison might be useful for the enquiry to suggest that he set out to show himself as non-threatening.

ⓐ Source B is useful for an enquiry into ....
....

ⓑ because it says/shows (information) ....
....

ⓒ This is useful because it suggests (inference) ....
....

③ Now complete the same process on a separate piece of paper for one piece of content selected from Source C on page 21.

One way of identifying useful content is to spot words or visual elements in the source that match words in the enquiry.

② How can I use nature and origin to evaluate usefulness?

Once you have selected content from each source and indicated that it could be useful to the enquiry, you need to evaluate **how** useful. Start by considering nature, origin and purpose (see page 22).

Considering the nature and origin of the source can highlight strengths or limitations that affect usefulness. The table below lists different criteria you can use in your evaluation.

① a Look at Source B on page 25. Tick ✓ one item from the criteria bank below that Source B meets strongly. This will be something that strengthens the source's usefulness.

b Cross out ~~cat~~ one criterion that Source B does not meet. This will be something that limits the source's usefulness.

Criteria	Questions to ask of the source	✓
Authoritativeness	Does the person who produced the source have the knowledge, or experience, to tell us about the enquiry?	
Typicality	Does the nature of the source allow us to get a representative, or complete, view of the enquiry topic?	
Objectivity	Do the perspective and purpose of the author/creator of the source affect the view it gives on the enquiry topic?	
Reliability	Are there reasons why the origin or nature of the source might make the source unreliable? (Note that an unreliable source is not necessarily less useful than a reliable one.)	

② Complete ✐ the table below for Source B, for an exam-style question asking: 'How useful is Source B for an enquiry into Hitler's change of approach for the Nazi Party after the Munich Putsch?'

Nature of source	How could the nature of the source affect its usefulness?	Origin of source	How could the origin of the source affect its usefulness?
Book published 1933		Prison warder/ later SS member	

③ A student has written the following evaluation of content from Source B.

> Source B is useful for an enquiry into Hitler's change of approach for the Nazi Party after the Munich Putsch because it suggests Hitler had decided in prison not to use violent methods for his 'National Movement' any more. Source B was written by a prison warder, which makes it more useful because he was an eyewitness who would have spoken to Hitler.

a What does the student use to evaluate the usefulness of the source content?

Circle Ⓐ your choice. | Nature | | Origin | | Purpose |

b The answer gives one result of the evaluation but does not explain it. Add this here. ✐
An eyewitness who would have spoken to Hitler is useful for this enquiry because:

....

c The student makes only one point about usefulness from their evaluation. Add one more. ✐

....

How can I use purpose to evaluate usefulness?

Purpose is why the source was written or created. It is another tool you can select for your evaluation of source content. You can use the criteria bank on page 26 to consider strengths and limitations of the content for the enquiry in the question.

Examples of purpose:

- a private diary written to record personal thoughts
- a propaganda poster created to persuade and influence
- a confidential government report written to communicate plans not discussed in public.

Source C Extract from a report on Hitler by the Bavarian police after Hitler applied for early release from Landsberg prison. Hitler was released on 20 December 1924.

The Headquarters urges that Hitler… should not be released. …

Many acts of violence by his followers, culminating in his putsch, are due entirely to his influence. With his energy he will without doubt encourage fresh public disturbances. He will be a permanent danger to the security of the state the moment he has been released. … Hitler will resume his ruthless struggle against the government and will not be afraid to break the law.

A student has selected the following content from Source C (above) to evaluate for usefulness for an enquiry into Hitler's change of approach for the Nazi Party after the Munich Putsch:

Source C is useful to the enquiry because it warns that Hitler will 'without doubt' try to use force against the government again if he is released from prison.

① What do you think the purpose of Source C was? Select ✓ your choice or choices.

A | To let Hitler know that the police were watching him. | ☐

B | To warn the authorities about the threat Hitler posed to the government. | ☐

C | To persuade the authorities not to release Hitler early. | ☐

② Suggest one way in which the purpose of Source C strengthens the usefulness of the source content for this enquiry. ✎

....

....

....

③ Suggest one way in which the purpose of Source C limits the usefulness of the source content for this enquiry. ✎

....

....

....

④ Now you have identified a strength and a limitation, you can make a judgement on 'how useful'. On a separate piece of paper, write ✎ an evaluation of Source C.

Students often only look for source weaknesses: make sure you also look for ways in which a source enhances usefulness.

Sample response

In this unit you have practised some skills relating to analysing sources for usefulness and evaluating them using provenance. Have a go at assessing and improving the following student answer to this exam-style question.

The sources for this question are on page 21.

Exam-style question

How useful are Sources B and C for an enquiry into reactions to Hitler's trial in 1924?

Source B shows Hitler saying his Putsch was not treason because it aimed to put right the betrayal of Germany in 1918. It is useful because it sets out Hitler's argument for why he was not guilty of treason and therefore we know what people who commented about the trial were reacting to. Because Source B is from a court trial, we know it would have been recorded accurately by someone in the court. That makes it more useful as we can be confident that Hitler really said this.

Source C shows the defendants in the trial. It is useful because it is a contemporary photo that helps us to see how Hitler, Ludendorff and others were represented in the media. This photo presents the men as important, serious and influential. However, the photo has been carefully posed to give this effect, so it is not an objective representation.

(1) Underline (A) and annotate (✏) where the student has considered nature, origin or purpose in their answer.

(2) Circle (A) each time the student evaluates a limitation of source usefulness.

(3) Double underline (A) each time the student evaluates a strength that improves source's usefulness.

(4) Does the student evaluate the usefulness of both sources? (A) [Yes] [No] [Not enough]

(5) Does the student make a judgement about 'how useful'? (A) [Yes] [No] [Not enough]

(6) Use your answers to (1)–(5) to advise this student how they could improve their answer. Make sure you include what is good about the student's answer as well as the ways in which their answer could be improved. (✏)

....

....

....

....

....

....

....

....

Your turn!

(1) Practise your skills of using provenance for evaluating the usefulness of two sources for an enquiry
with the following exam-style question. Use the work you have done on the two sources through this
unit to help you. Continue on a separate piece of paper if you need to. ✎

Exam-style question

How useful are Sources B and C for an enquiry into Hitler's change of approach for
the Nazi Party after the Munich Putsch?

Source B *From a book written by Otto Lurker called* Hitler Behind Prison Bars, *which was published in 1933.
Lurker was a warder at Landsberg prison when Hitler was imprisoned there in 1924. He later joined the SS.*

Hitler has shown himself to be an orderly, disciplined prisoner… He makes no exceptional demands, is calm and sensible,
serious, in no way aggressive. … He is without personal vanity, is content with the prison diet, neither smokes not drinks. …
Hitler will undoubtedly try to revive enthusiasm for the National Movement as he sees it; he will not, however, employ his
previous violent methods. … I have no hesitation in saying that Hitler's general behaviour under detention merits the grant of a
probationary period.

Source C *Extract from a report on Hitler by the Bavarian police after Hitler applied for early release
from Landsberg prison. Hitler was released on 20 December 1924.*

The Headquarters urges that Hitler… should not be released. …

Many acts of violence by his followers, culminating in his putsch, are due entirely to his influence. With his energy he will
without doubt encourage fresh public disturbances. He will be a permanent danger to the security of the state the moment he
has been released. … Hitler will resume his ruthless struggle against the government and will not be afraid to break the law.

Remember:
- analyse both sources to select potentially useful content
- always link your analysis to 'how useful' for the enquiry
- consider N, O and/or P for your evaluation of the potentially useful content
- you do not need to use N, O and P each time: select the aspects of provenance
  that work best in deciding 'how useful'
- refer to the criteria bank on page 26 when considering strengths and limitations
- make a judgement about usefulness using your strengths and limitations evaluations.

Continue your answer on a separate piece of paper if you need to: there will be more
space on the exam paper than is provided here.

Review your skills

Check up

Review your response to the exam-style question on page 29. Tick ✓ the column to show how well you think you have done each of the following.

	Had a go ✓	Nearly there ✓	Got it! ✓
analysed both sources to identify potentially useful content for the enquiry	☐	☐	☐
used N, O and/or P to evaluate usefulness of content from both sources	☐	☐	☐
made a judgement about usefulness of both sources	☐	☐	☐

Look over all of your work in this unit. Note down 🖉 the three most important things to remember about how best to evaluate sources using provenance.

① ....

② ....

③ ....

Need more practice?

If you want to practise another exam-style question, try 🖉 the one below. It relates to a different topic – challenges to the Weimar Republic – but the skills you need to use are just the same. The sources you need to complete this question can be found on page 81.

> **Exam-style question**
>
> How useful are Sources B and C for an enquiry into challenges to the Weimar Republic from the extreme left and right?

How confident do you feel about each of these **skills**? Colour in 🖉 the bars.

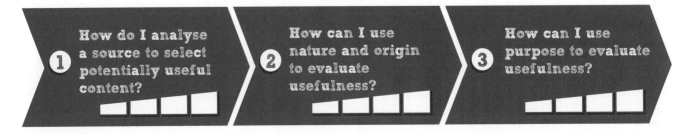

1 How do I analyse a source to select potentially useful content?

2 How can I use nature and origin to evaluate usefulness?

3 How can I use purpose to evaluate usefulness?

④ Using your own knowledge to decide how useful a source is

This unit enhances your skills in using your knowledge for evaluating source usefulness (see Unit 3 for using NOP to do this). The skills you will build are how to:

- use your own knowledge to help you select potentially useful content
- use your own knowledge to evaluate strengths and limitations of source usefulness
- make a judgement from your evaluation.

Here is another source utility question.

Exam-style question

Study Sources B and C.

How useful are Sources B and C for an enquiry into the impact of unemployment in the years 1929–33?

Explain your answer, using Sources B and C and your knowledge of the historical context. **(8 marks)**

Source B   *A graph of unemployment figures using data from the* International Labour Review *for the years 1929–33. The* International Labour Review *is a trusted academic journal reporting on industry.*

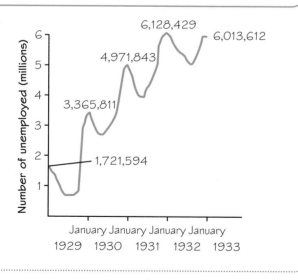

Source C   *From an interview with Frau Mundt in the 1960s. She is recalling her life as a child in the early 1930s.*

In 1930 the banks failed. All of a sudden, all credit was due. No one had any money. Everything gone. Do you know what that means? I own nothing. No money, no work, no food. Seven marks a week as unemployed. Families with two children, ten children and more, seven marks. And then came 1932. My mother and father went and heard Adolf Hitler. The next morning they told us what he had for goals, for ideas, how he was on the side of the unemployed. My mother wept for joy. My parents prayed dear God give this man all the votes so that we could get out of need. There was no one else who promised what he did.

The three key questions in the **skills boosts** will help you to evaluate how useful and reliable a source is.

① How do I use my knowledge to select potentially useful content?

② How do I use my knowledge to evaluate for usefulness?

③ How do I make a judgement on 'how useful'?

There are different routes to tackling 'how useful' questions. Practise using them when you are answering a 'how useful' question, but remember that not all of them will apply to every source.

---

1 Read the question

The exam question will always ask 'how useful' a source is 'for an enquiry into' something particular. For example, the question on page 31 is 'how useful… for an enquiry into the impact of unemployment in the years 1929–33?'

The 'for an enquiry into' information provides your focus for answering the 'how useful' question.

---

2 Source content

Select content from the source that could potentially be useful for the enquiry. For example, Source B on page 31 provides specific data about the rise in unemployment between 1929 and 1933.

---

3 NOP

Evaluate the content you have selected from each source to identify the strengths and limitations of its usefulness. One option is to consider nature, origin and/or purpose (see Unit 3) first. Then use your own knowledge to make your evaluation stronger.

---

4 Contextual knowledge

Contextual knowledge is the knowledge you already have about the enquiry focus. It allows you to evaluate the usefulness of source content by considering what it adds to our understanding and its accuracy, and what it leaves out. You can use your contextual knowledge in several different ways (although not all of them will apply to every source), including:

- to understand the position of the origin of the source (e.g. are they in a unique position?)
- to understand the position or the attitudes of the source's audience
- to evaluate the accuracy of what is said in the source
- to evaluate how typical the source is, and what that says about how useful it is
- to be aware of what is missing that weakens the evidence provided by the source.

---

5 Make a judgement

Your evaluation of each source should end with a judgement about how useful the source is for the enquiry. Base your judgement on the strengths and limitations identified by your evaluation.

---

(1) Read the exam-style question on page 31. What is the enquiry of the question?

....

(2) Consider Source B on page 31. Use NOP to identify one strength of Source B: something that makes it useful to the enquiry focus.

....

....

....

....

The growth of unemployment – its causes and impact

This unit uses the theme of the causes and impact of the growth of unemployment 1929–33 to build your skills in evaluating a source's usefulness. If you need to review your knowledge of this theme, work through these pages.

① Fill in 🖉 the gaps in this student answer about why unemployment in Germany jumped from 1.3 million in September 1929 to 6.1 million in January 1933, by writing the phrases from the boxes below in the correct spaces.

The main reason for the rapid rise in unemployment was an economic collapse following the .... in the USA in October 1929. Falling .... on the Wall Street stock exchange triggered the crash as people tried to sell their shares before they lost too much value. On 'Black Thursday', ..., panic selling meant investors lost $4 billion.

German banks were .... in US shares, and suffered huge losses. As people heard of the banks' losses, they rushed to try to withdraw their savings before the banks .... In order to stay in business, banks told .... that loans had to be repaid. Without the ...., German industries and farms closed, or, at best, cut back on production. Many Germans lost their jobs. As people became poorer, they ...., which meant German industries sold fewer products, and had to reduce production even more, increasing the ....

---

numbers of unemployed	major investors	24 October 1929
Wall Street Crash	cut back on their spending	ran out of money
German industries and farms	loans they depended on	share prices

② The sentences below are about the impacts of unemployment on the German people in the years 1929–33. Only one of each pair is true. Tick ✓ the sentences you think are correct.

A | As the number of unemployed grew, the government raised taxes so it could pay out unemployment benefits to everyone affected. This reduced suffering considerably. | ☐

B | As the number of unemployed grew, the government could not afford to pay unemployment benefits. In response it cut benefits and raised taxes, increasing suffering. | ☐

C | Many unemployed people struggled to pay their rent and became homeless. Shanty towns sprang up, filled with unemployed people desperate for work or food. | ☐

D | Many unemployed people struggled to pay their rent and became homeless. The government provided shanty towns for them to live in, rent free. | ☐

E | The unemployment crisis had one positive result: the moderate parties in the Reichstag put aside their difficulties and worked together to minimise people's suffering. | ☐

F | The moderate parties on the left and the right objected to Brüning's policies. Brüning was forced to govern by decree, undermining confidence in the Weimar government. | ☐

③ Complete ✏ this table of Reichstag general election results by filling in the names of the political parties.

General elections, 1929–32: seats in the Reichstag			
Political parties	May 1928	September 1930	July 1932
	152	143	133
	12	107	230
	54	77	89

④ Study Source A. Write ✏ 'T' or 'F' beside the comments below to show whether they are true or false.

Source A *A poster from the KPD (Communist Party) for the Reichstag election of 1932. The words at the bottom of the poster say 'End this system'.*

a The poster shows a large red man with a raised fist. He represents German farmers. ☐

b The large red man has thin, sunken cheeks to show that the workers are hungry and exhausted. ☐

c The caption on the poster says 'End this system'. It means the workers should smash the capitalist system that keeps them poor and makes them unemployed. ☐

d The figures around the table represent the leaders of the KPD, discussing how best to solve the problems facing the Republic. ☐

1 How do I use my knowledge to select potentially useful content?

If you use context knowledge to support an inference (see page 25), you are already demonstrating a strength of the source.

Exam-style question

How useful is Source B for an enquiry into the growth in support for extremist parties after the Wall Street Crash (1929)?

Source B

From the memoirs of Lea Grundig, written in 1964. Lea Grundig was the daughter of a German Jewish merchant and a member of the German Communist Party in the 1920s and 1930s. Here she remembers conditions in 1932.

Who was to blame for 6 million unemployed? Where did this unbelievable misery come from? 'The Jews are to blame!' they screamed in chorus. 'The lost war!' 'The Reds with their stab in the back!'

'Capitalism' said the Communists, and they were right. 'Because only a few people own all the machines and the factories and have them work only for their profit. Meanwhile, the workers who actually produce everything cannot afford to buy anything. We must put an end to the exploitation. We must have socialism.'

Socialism. Like a great bell of ancient longing, that's how this word sounded.

① Read this extract from the first part of a student's answer to the question above.

  a Underline Ⓐ where the student is making an inference from the source about usefulness.

  b Circle Ⓐ where the student is using their own knowledge to support the inference.

> Source B suggests that workers were attracted to the KPD because while they could not afford to buy anything, factory owners stayed rich. It is true that even those who still had jobs in 1932 faced falling income because employers tried to save money by cutting wages. This is useful because this unfairness explains reasons for growing support for the KPD.

Making a list (or drawing a spider diagram) of connections to the enquiry from your own knowledge will help to prepare you to look out for relevant content in the sources.

② Here is a spider diagram jotted down by a student. Can you add any more connections of your own?

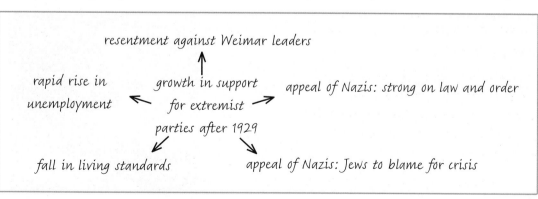

③ Use the completed spider diagram to make another inference from this source, using your own knowledge. Write ✎ your answer on a separate piece of paper.

Unit 4 Using your own knowledge to decide how useful a source is   35

② How do I use my knowledge to evaluate for usefulness?

In Unit 3 you used N, O and/or P to evaluate source content for usefulness. You can also use your knowledge of the historical context to identify strengths and weaknesses of source usefulness.

It is very important that your contextual knowledge is linked to the evaluation of the sources. If no link is made, no marks can be awarded.

① Study Source B and this student answer to the exam-style question on page 35.

> Source B says that the workers 'cannot afford to buy anything'. This would be useful for the enquiry because it would suggest that one reason for increasing support for extremist parties like the KPD was that workers were desperate because they could not afford to live. One problem with the source is that the author was a member of the Communist Party, which could affect its objectivity about the appeal of socialism, but it is true that wages were cut so that in 1932 they were 30% lower than in 1928, supporting the claim that even people in work could become desperate. That suggests that Source B makes a useful contribution to the enquiry.

When you are assessing the usefulness of a source using your own knowledge of the historical context, consider strengths or limitations.
- Strengths are when your own knowledge can confirm the accuracy (and so the reliability) of what the source says.
- Limitations are when a source does not address something important about the enquiry focus that you would expect it to.

a Highlight 🖉 where the student makes an inference about the source content.

b Underline Ⓐ where the student identifies a limitation of the source content's usefulness. Which evaluation tool do they use for this: N, O, P or historical knowledge? Double underline Ⓐ your choice.

c Circle Ⓐ where the student identifies a strength of the source content's usefulness. Which evaluation tool do they use for this: N, O, P or historical knowledge? Circle Ⓐ your choice.

d Does the answer make a judgement about usefulness? Ⓐ | Yes | | No |

② In the answer above, the student has identified a strength of the source using their knowledge of historical context. Tick ✓ the option below that is a valid weakness of the source, based on the enquiry focus and your knowledge of historical context.

A | 'Unbelievable misery' suggests that conditions were very hard for workers in 1932. | ☐

B | The author of the source had been a member of the KPD since the 1920s, which makes the source less useful – she was not 'converted' to communism by the experiences after 1929. | ☐

C | The growth in extremism after 1929 also happened because people could see that the government parties had no answer to the crisis. The source does not mention this. | ☐

D | The source describes how Communist theory explained the crisis in a way that made sense to working people in Germany at the time. | ☐

③ Which of the remaining options: 🖉

a is an inference, not an assessment? ....

b is about provenance, not content? ....

c is describing a strength, not a weakness? ....

No source can include everything, but if a source seems to be leaving out an important aspect of content that you know is relevant to the enquiry, you can use this historical knowledge in your evaluation as a limitation of its usefulness.

③ How do I make a judgement on 'how useful'?

Use your evaluation of the strengths and limitations of each source to make a judgement about how useful it is for the enquiry.

Study this exam-style question and its two sources, then complete the activity that follows.

The sources you need to complete this question can be found on page 81.

Exam-style question

Study Sources B and C.

How useful are Sources B and C for an enquiry into the use of concentration camps for political prisoners in the 1930s?

Explain your answer, using Sources B and C and your knowledge of the historical context.   **(8 marks)**

① The statements below describe some strengths and weaknesses of Sources B and C, which you can use in evaluating them both for usefulness: but which belongs to which? Write ✐ B or C next to each statement to show your choices.

Source B or C?	Statement	Strength or weakness?
	i 4,000 Communists were arrested in March 1933 in Berlin	
	ii Nature strengthens usefulness, as written in private to friends	
	iii Nazi propaganda did claim that concentration camps were for 're-education'	
	iv In the November 1933 election, 92% of votes were for the NSDAP	
	v Sources written by opponents of Nazism may not give typical views	
	vi Purpose possibly limits usefulness because written to shock	

② Now decide which are strengths and which are weaknesses. Write ✐ 'strength' or 'weakness' in column 3. A source with more strengths than weaknesses is likely to be useful to the enquiry.

③ Use the following statements to judge how useful B and C are to the enquiry on this page. Write ✐ your answer on a separate piece of paper.

Source B suggests that thousands of the Nazis' political opponents were put into concentration camps in 1933 and tortured.

Source C suggests that some Germans approved of putting Communists and Social Democrats into concentration camps for re-education.

Sample response

A good answer to the 'how useful' question will make judgements about usefulness for the enquiry in the question. These judgements are based on the evaluation of source content for usefulness using provenance and your own knowledge of the historical context.

Consider one student's response to the following question. The sources for this question are on page 81.

Exam-style question

Study Sources B and C.

How useful are Sources B and C for an enquiry into the use of concentration camps for political prisoners in the 1930s?

Explain your answer, using Sources B and C and your knowledge of the historical context.   **(8 marks)**

The Nazis used fear of a Communist uprising following the Reichstag Fire (February 1933) to increase their popularity. This included arresting KPD supporters and Social Democrats. Source C is useful in helping explain why many Germans supported this, even though people were arrested and imprisoned without trial – many Germans were frightened of Communists and wanted a strong government to 'clean up' Germany. Because Source C is from private letters it is probably reliable at setting out how the author really felt about the use of concentration camps.

Source B is about opposition to the use of concentration camps. It suggests that the SA were very brutal and even murderous in the way they treated KPD and SPD prisoners. This is useful because at the time the Nazi government said that prisoners were not mistreated. They even allowed journalists to visit some concentration camps to show this. Source B was designed to convince people about 'Hitler's Crimes', which could affect its reliability as a source. However, it was dangerous to express negative opinions about the Nazis, which makes sources such as Source B very rare. That makes Source B very useful for this enquiry.

Both sources are therefore useful to the enquiry. In my view Source B is the most useful, because it is so rare to have sources from groups opposing the Nazi regime.

---

① ⓐ Underline Ⓐ where the student assesses usefulness using provenance (NOP).

   ⓑ Circle Ⓐ where the student uses their own knowledge of the historical context to assess usefulness.

   ⓒ Double underline Ⓐ where the student makes a judgement or judgements about usefulness.

   > You do not need to make a comparison between the sources and there are no marks available for doing this.

② Use the following list to evaluate the student's answer. ✓

Lower level	✓	Higher level	✓
Judgements about usefulness are made but they are not specific to the enquiry		The judgements are about usefulness to the specific enquiry in the question	
Provenance is used to evaluate usefulness in relation to N, O and/or P		Contextual knowledge is used to evaluate the strength of N, O and/or P (e.g. to understand the position of O)	
Contextual knowledge is included, but not used directly to evaluate strengths or weaknesses		Contextual knowledge is used directly to evaluate content by confirming accuracy of source information or identifying important gaps in source information	

Your turn!

(1) Now you are going to write ✏ your own response to the exam-style question at the start of this unit.

Exam-style question

Study Sources B and C.

How useful are Sources B and C for an enquiry into the impact of unemployment in the years 1929–33?

Explain your answer, using Sources B and C and your knowledge of the historical context. **(8 marks)**

The sources for this question are on page 31.

You can use the following table to help you plan your answer, which you should write ✏ on a separate piece of paper.

	Source B	Source C
Enquiry focus: useful for what?		
Usefulness from provenance: Strengths: Limitations:		
Usefulness from knowledge of historical context: More useful because: Less useful because:		
Number of strengths		
Number of limitations		
Judgement		

Remember to:

- select potentially useful content from both sources to evaluate for usefulness
- suggest inferences from the content that show the link to usefulness to the enquiry
- use provenance to evaluate the usefulness of the sources' content for the enquiry
- use your knowledge of historical context to evaluate the usefulness of the sources' content and provenance – your contextual knowledge must be linked to the evaluation of the sources
- include judgements about 'how useful' each source is to the enquiry.

Review your skills

Check up

Review your response to the exam-style question on page 39. Tick ✓ the column to show how well you think you have done each of the following.

	Had a go ✓	Nearly there ✓	Got it! ✓
used historical context knowledge to evaluate inferences	☐	☐	☐
used provenance to evaluate usefulness	☐	☐	☐
used historical context knowledge to evaluate usefulness	☐	☐	☐
made judgements about 'how useful' for each source	☐	☐	☐

Look over all of your work in this unit. Note down ✐ the three most important things to remember about how best to use your knowledge to decide how useful a source is.

① ....

② ....

③ ....

Need more practice?

If you want to practise another exam-style question, try ✐ the exam-style question below. The sources you need to complete this question can be found on page 82.

Exam-style question

Study Sources B and C.

How useful are Sources B and C for an enquiry into the way Hitler undermined democracy in 1933?

Explain your answer, using Sources B and C and your knowledge of the historical context.   **(8 marks)**

How confident do you feel about each of these **skills**? Colour in ✐ the bars.

1 How do I use my knowledge to select potentially useful content?

2 How do I use my knowledge to evaluate for usefulness?

3 How do I make a judgement on 'how useful'?

⑤ Identifying the difference between interpretations

This unit will help you to identify the difference between interpretations. The skills you will build are how to:

- analyse different interpretations
- identify the main difference between two interpretations
- support your answer with relevant details from the interpretations.

The following exam-style question is worth 4 marks. It is important to deal with it efficiently so that you can maximise your time on higher-value questions. The pattern of the question is as follows.

Exam-style question

Study Interpretations 1 and 2. They give different views about Nazi persecution of the Jews.

What is the main difference between these views?

Explain your answer, using details from both interpretations.   **(4 marks)**

Interpretation 1   *From* Years of Weimar, the Third Reich and Post-War Germany, *by David Evans and Jane Jenkins, published in 2008.*

Nazi propaganda failed to encourage hatred against the Jews, apart from on special occasions such as *Kristallnacht*. German people had different opinions about Jews, from those who feared the Jews, to those who refused to hate people because of their race, because it was morally wrong. Although constant propaganda against the Jews did not succeed in making people hate them, there was a widespread lack of interest in what happened to the Jews. It was this lack of interest which allowed the Nazis to keep developing their policy of racial hatred and extermination.

Interpretation 2   *From* The Weimar Republic and Nazi Germany *by Warren B. Morris, Jr., published in 1982.*

The anti-Jewish frenzy intensified in 1935. Nazis organised new boycotts of Jewish businesses and used force to keep Jews from attending theatres, swimming pools, or other public places. Whole towns fell under the influence of the fanaticism and posted signs prohibiting Jews from entering their districts. The campaign reached its height during the Nazi party rally at Nuremberg on 15 September 1935, where, to a crowd of cheering admirers, Hitler announced the Nuremberg Laws.

The three key questions in the **skills boosts** will help you to analyse interpretations and identify and explain a main difference between two interpretations.

 1 How do I analyse different interpretations?

2 How do I identify the main difference between interpretations?

 3 How do I refer back to the interpretations to support my answer?

This type of exam question is essentially about spotting the difference between two views. You need to find a key difference rather than a superficial one. The two interpretations in the exam will always have been selected so that there is a key difference to spot.

Read the following two views about the difficulties of explaining the Nazi persecution of minorities.

A ⓘ

Providing a single, clear explanation for the horrors of Nazism is impossible, however much we might like to find one. This is such a complex topic and there is so much research on Weimar and Nazi Germany that no one historian could ever expect to be an expert on all of it. The different theories about what happened in Weimar and Nazi Germany are often very complex and change with each new generation of historians. The best an historian can do is hope to contribute to a more complete understanding of the period.

B ⓘ

Understanding reasons for the Nazi persecutions is difficult because the Nazis destroyed police records during the Second World War. However, some police archives were not destroyed and historians have uncovered convincing evidence that the persecution of minorities by the Nazis happened because ordinary Germans supported it. The reason for this support was usually because ordinary Germans benefited in some way from the persecution, for example because they wanted to get rid of a business rival.

① Tick ✓ the statement below that describes the main difference between the two views.

A | View A is about Weimar and Nazi Germany while View B is only about Nazi Germany. | ☐

B | View A says that no one could expect to be an expert on all of the research about Weimar and Nazi Germany, while View B doesn't say that. | ☐

C | View A says the Nazi persecution of minorities is impossible to explain because German history is too complicated to understand, while View B says Nazi persecution is impossible to understand because none of the sources are reliable. | ☐

D | View A says it is impossible to give a single explanation for Nazi persecution, while View B suggests it is possible to explain why Nazi persecution happened. | ☐

② Now try to spot the difference between another two views. Write ✎ your answer below.

C ⓘ

Students who do well at this exam question focus on identifying a main difference between the interpretations and add details from both interpretations to support their answer.

D ⓘ

Students often do very well at this exam question, identifying a main difference and supporting that difference with details from both interpretations, but because they spend too much time on it they then have less time than they need for higher-mark questions.

The main difference between these two views is ....

....

....

The persecution of minorities

This unit uses the theme of Nazi persecution of minorities to build your skills in identifying a main difference between interpretations. If you need to review your knowledge of this theme, work through these pages.

1 Draw ✏ lines to link these terms about Nazi racial beliefs and policies to their correct definitions.

A Eugenics	**a** An ancient group of Northern Europeans who the Nazis believed to be the master race: the best of all human races.
B Aryan race	**b** The idea that the Aryan race should be kept 'pure' by avoiding any breeding with other, inferior races. Laws were passed against mixed-race marriages.
C *Herrenvolk*	**c** 'Sub-humans': people considered racially inferior by the Nazis, for example Slavs and Jews.
D Racial hygiene	**d** Studying ways of improving human abilities, e.g. by selecting the 'best' parents or by preventing 'unsuitable' people from having children.
E *Untermenschen*	**e** The 'master race'. Hitler and the Nazis believed this was the Aryan race.

2 A student has written the following paragraph about the Nazi treatment of minorities. There are three factual errors in the paragraph that would weaken it. Cross them out (~~cat~~), then write ✏ corrections on the lines provided below.

> The Nazis believed the Roma were Untermenschen and that gave the Germanic race the right to take land from them to the east of Germany to allow the Germans 'Lebensraum', which meant living space. Another minority persecuted by the Nazis were the Roma. In 1939 preparations started to deport all Roma from Germany. A third minority persecuted by the Nazis were homosexuals. In 1935 the Nazis made it illegal to be gay and started putting homosexuals in prison. It is thought that between 1933 and 1945 approximately 100,000 men had been arrested for homosexuality. People with disabilities were also persecuted by the Nazis. In 1939 the Nazis brought in the Law for the Prevention of Hereditarily Diseased Offspring, which made it compulsory for people who were mentally ill, alcoholic, deaf, blind, deformed or epileptic to be sterilised.

Correction 1: ....

....

Correction 2: ....

....

Correction 3: ....

....

3 Put the stages in the Nazi persecution of the Jews in chronological order by numbering ✎ the statements below 1–8, with 1 being the earliest. The first is done for you.

A | Official boycott of all Jewish businesses, doctors and lawyers. | **1**

B | Jews banned from government jobs; Jewish teachers and civil servants. | ☐

C | *Kristallnacht* – after which Jews were fined 1 billion marks for the damage. | ☐

D | Orders given to evict all Jews from their homes and assemble them ready for deportation from Germany. | ☐

E | Jews banned from inheriting land. | ☐

F | Jews banned from the army. | ☐

G | Jews had to carry identity cards. | ☐

H | The Nuremberg Laws: Jews lost citizenship rights, had to wear yellow stars, and were forbidden from marrying or having sexual relations with German citizens. | ☐

4 Read the following statements about *Kristallnacht* and tick ✓ the ones you think are true.

a | *Kristallnacht* happened after a Polish Jew shot a Nazi official. | ☐

b | *Kristallnacht* happened the year before the Berlin Olympic Games. | ☐

c | The Nazis openly encouraged people to attack synagogues and Jewish businesses. | ☐

d | *Kristallnacht* means 'Crystal Night', after the broken glass of smashed windows. | ☐

e | The police were ordered not to stop violence against Jews by members of the public. | ☐

f | Although 814 shops, 171 homes and 191 synagogues were destroyed, no one was killed. | ☐

g | Although Jews were made to pay for the damage of *Kristallnacht*, they were allowed to claim for it through their insurance policies. | ☐

5 Complete this passage about the Nuremberg Laws by writing ✎ words or phrases from the box below in the correct gaps.

The Nuremberg Laws were passed on 15 September .... during the Nazis' party congress in .... There were .... : the Reich Citizenship Law and the Reich Law for the Protection of German Blood and Honour. Under the Reich Citizenship Law, only those of German .... could be German .... Jews became German ...., not citizens, which meant they no longer had the .... or hold German passports, among other things. Under the Reich Law for the Protection of German Blood and Honour, Jews were forbidden from .... German citizens or having sexual relations with German citizens. German citizens who were already married to Jews were encouraged to .... them.

| Nuremberg | right to vote | blood | marrying | citizens |
| divorce | 1935 | 'subjects' | yellow patch | two laws |

1 How do I analyse different interpretations?

Analysing the two interpretations means working out what view they are each giving about a topic. The question tells you what the interpretations are giving different views about.

There will always be a main difference between the two interpretations on the exam paper, and key 'opinion' words or phrases in the texts will often highlight different points of view. For example, one interpretation could give a positive view while the other could give a negative view.

① Use the key words in the boxes to create two different interpretations of the Nazi persecution of the Jews from the following identical texts.

| frequently | Because | not supported | clear | praised |

Interpretation 1: .... the Nazi regime constantly promoted the persecution of the Jews, the German people .... took an active part in persecution. For example, after Kristallnacht ordinary Germans .... the SA's destruction of Jewish shops and synagogues. It was .... that ordinary Germans supported the persecution. The view that Germans were too intimidated to oppose the Nazi regime is .... by the evidence.

| rarely | While | supported | never clear | criticised |

Interpretation 2: .... the Nazi regime constantly promoted the persecution of the Jews, the German people .... took an active part in persecution. For example, after Kristallnacht ordinary Germans .... the SA's destruction of Jewish shops and synagogues. It was .... that ordinary Germans supported the persecution. The view that Germans were too intimidated to oppose the Nazi regime is .... by the evidence.

② Below are two short extracts from two interpretations of Nazi persecution of the Jews (the full interpretations are on page 46).

- **Interpretation 1**: Now, with hindsight, we can see a step-by-step path to total annihilation [of the Jews], but this was not clear at the time.
- **Interpretation 2**: Hitler's purpose was plain and unchanging… He meant to carry out the extermination of the Jewish race in Europe.

a Underline Ⓐ the key 'opinion' words in each extract.

b Circle Ⓐ a single key word or phrase that you feel represents each extract.

c Briefly summarise in your own words what each interpretation is saying. Use the key words to help you.

Interpretation 1: ....

....

Interpretation 2: ....

....

② How do I identify the main difference between interpretations?

The question will always tell you what the interpretations are giving different views about. Compare the interpretations' views to spot the difference between them.

Consider this exam-style question and the interpretations that follow it.

Exam-style question

Study Interpretations 1 and 2. They give different views about the Nazi persecution of the Jews.

What is the main difference between these views?

Interpretation 1 *From Hitler's Germany, by Roderick Stackelberg, published in 1999.*

There was <u>no master plan</u> for how the destruction of the Jewish community in Germany was to be accomplished. Throughout the 1930s persecution, isolation, and degradation of the Jews proceeded <u>fitfully</u> [not regularly] <u>through various stages</u>, thus repeatedly raising hopes in the Jewish community that the worst was finally over. Now, <u>with hindsight</u>, we can see a <u>step-by-step path</u> to total annihilation, but this was <u>not clear at the time</u>. People <u>could not foresee</u> the terrible end of the process.

Interpretation 2 *From Hitler: a study in tyranny by Alan Bullock, published in 1962.*

Hitler's purpose was plain and unchanging, from his speeches in 1922 through *Kristallnacht* to the death camps. He meant to carry out the extermination of the Jewish race in Europe, using the word 'extermination' not in a theoretical way but as something that the German state should actually do – and he very largely succeeded. At least four million Jews perished in Europe under Hitler's rule – apart from the number driven from their homes who succeeded in finding refuge abroad. History records few, if any, crimes that are so enormous and carried out with such cold-blooded purpose.

① A student has underlined key 'opinion' terms suggesting a point of view in Interpretation 1.
Do the same for Interpretation 2. Ⓐ

② This table lists three views from Interpretation 1 in one column. In the other, write ✏ in views from Interpretation 2 that do not agree. You can use the same view more than once.

Interpretation 1's view	Interpretation 2's view
<u>No master plan</u>	
Persecution proceeded <u>fitfully, through various stages</u>	
<u>Step-by-step path to total annihilation not clear at the time</u>	

③ Using the table, identify the main difference between the two interpretations. Write ✏ your answer here. Be concise.

....

....

③ How do I refer back to the interpretations to support my answer?

Once you have identified the main difference between the two interpretations, you need to add details from the interpretations to support your answer.

This question is worth 4 marks, so your answer can be concise. You could consider following a process like this to tackle this question:

- Underline key 'opinion' words in each interpretation as you read it.

- Write down your main difference: 'The main difference is that Interpretation 1 [...] while Interpretation 2 [...].

- Use your highlighting to pick out supporting detail. Add this to your answer: For example, 'Interpretation 1 says [...] while Interpretation 2 says [...]'.

① Read the following student response to the exam-style question below. The interpretations for this question are on page 46.

   ⓐ Double underline Ⓐ the supporting detail in the student's response below.

   ⓑ Tick ✓ where the supporting detail contains text you had also underlined as key 'opinion' words.

Exam-style question

Study Interpretations 1 and 2. They give different views about the Nazi persecution of the Jews.

What is the main difference between these views?

> The main difference is that Interpretation 2 says it was always clear that the Nazis were going to exterminate the Jews, while Interpretation 1 says it was not always clear. For example, Interpretation 2 says Hitler's purpose was 'plain and unchanging', while Interpretation 1 says there was 'no master plan'.

Avoid spending too much time describing a difference: identify it clearly and concisely, use precisely selected detail to back up your answer, and then move on.

② A student has written an answer to the exam-style question above.

   ⓐ The student has written more than is needed in the first part of their answer. Use the process shown in the bullet points above to decide what is important to keep in this answer, and cross out ~~(cat)~~ everything else.

   ⓑ The student has not included detail to back up their answer for one of the interpretations. Add relevant detail below to complete ✐ the answer.

> There is a main difference between the interpretations which is to do with whether the Nazis always intended their persecution of the Jews to end in the extermination of the Jews in Europe or whether this happened not according to a definite plan. Interpretation 1 says it was not clear at the time that Nazi persecution of the Jewish community in Germany was leading to the extermination of the Jews, while Interpretation 2 says it was always clear that Hitler meant to exterminate the Jews from the start not just of his rule over Germany but ever since the early 1920s. For example, Interpretation 1 says a 'step-by-step path to annihilation... was not clear at the time'.

....

....

Sample response

Read the two student answers to the following exam-style question (the interpretations are on page 46).
Then complete the activity that comes after it.

Exam-style question

Study Interpretations 1 and 2. They give different views about the Nazi persecution of the Jews.

What is the main difference between these views?

Answer A

Interpretation 2 was written a long time before Interpretation 1 so it won't be as accurate because the

author wouldn't know as much detail. For example, Interpretation 2 says that 4 million Jews died in the

Holocaust, when it was actually 6 million.

Answer B

The main difference is about whether the Nazis always planned to exterminate the Jews: Interpretation 1

says no, Interpretation 2 says yes.

---

1. In each answer, circle (A) where the student shows they have identified the main difference (if they
   have done this).

2. Underline (A) in each answer where the student has supported their answer with detail from the
   interpretations (if they have done this).

3. Which answer do you think is better? Explain (✏) your opinion here.

   ....

   ....

   ....

   ....

4. Now write (✏) your own answer to the question. You can use strong points from the answers above,
   and improve on their weaknesses.

   ....

   ....

   ....

   ....

   ....

   ....

> Analyse the interpretations to identify a key difference of view.
> Use your analysis to select supporting detail to back up your answer.
> Be concise: don't write more description or more supporting detail than you need to.

Your turn!

1. Here is the exam-style question and the interpretations from the start of this unit. Use this question to practise your efficient analysis technique so that you can identify and write ✏️ a main difference and add supporting detail in around 5–6 minutes.

Exam-style question

Study Interpretations 1 and 2. They give different views about the Nazi persecution of the Jews.

What is the main difference between these views?

Interpretation 1

From Years of Weimar, the Third Reich and Post-War Germany, *by David Evans and Jane Jenkins, published in 2008.*

<u>Nazi propaganda failed to encourage hatred against the Jews</u>, apart from on special occasions such as *Kristallnacht*. German people had different opinions about Jews, from those who feared the Jews, to those who refused to hate people because of their race, because it was morally wrong. Although constant propaganda against the Jews did not succeed in making people hate them, <u>there was a widespread lack of interest in what happened to the Jews</u>. It was this lack of interest which allowed the Nazis to keep developing their policy of racial hatred and extermination.

Interpretation 2

From The Weimar Republic and Nazi Germany, *by Warren B. Morris, Jr., published in 1982.*

<u>The anti-Jewish frenzy</u> intensified in 1935. Nazis organised new boycotts of Jewish businesses and used force to keep Jews from attending theatres, swimming pools, or other public places. <u>Whole towns fell under the influence of the fanaticism</u> and posted signs prohibiting Jews from entering their districts. The campaign reached its height during the Nazi party rally at Nuremberg on 15 September 1935, where, to a crowd of cheering admirers, Hitler announced the Nuremberg Laws.

A student has already underlined parts of the interpretations to help identify the main difference.

Remember:
- the question tells you what the difference is about
- analysis of key words/phrases helps to unlock the difference and gives you options for your selection of precise supporting detail
- your answer can be concise: a maximum of 4 marks is available
- state the main difference and then support it with detail from both interpretations.

Review your skills

Check up

Review your response to the exam-style question on page 49. Tick ✓ the column to show how well you think you have done each of the following.

	Had a go ✓	Nearly there ✓	Got it! ✓
identified the main difference	☐	☐	☐
supported the main difference with details from the interpretations	☐	☐	☐

Look over all of your work in this unit. Note down ✏ the three most important things to remember about how best to identify the difference between interpretations.

① ....

② ....

③ ....

Need more practice?

If you want to practise another exam-style question, try ✏ the one below. The interpretations are on page 82.

Exam-style question

Study Interpretations 1 and 2. They give different views about the Weimar Constitution.

What is the main difference between these views?

Explain your answer, using details from both interpretations.

(4 marks)

How confident do you feel about each of these **skills**? Colour in ✏ the bars.

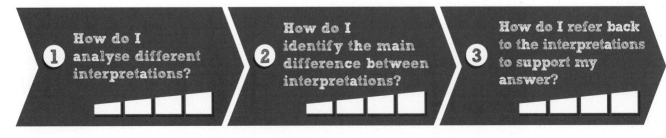

① How do I analyse different interpretations?

② How do I identify the main difference between interpretations?

③ How do I refer back to the interpretations to support my answer?

⑥ Suggesting a reason why interpretations give different views

This unit will help you to suggest a reason why interpretations give different views. The skills you will build are how to:

- explain difference in interpretations by looking at evidence from the period
- understand the historians' emphasis to explain difference
- apply the wider historical context to explain difference.

This unit is about questions like the one below. (Sources B and C are on page 52.)

Exam-style question

Suggest **one** reason why Interpretations 1 and 2 give different views about Nazi policies to reduce unemployment.

You may use Sources B and C to help explain your answer.

(4 marks)

Interpretation 1

From Years of Weimar and the Third Reich, *by David Evans and Jane Jenkins, published in 1999.*

Many people came to feel a sense of pride in Germany's future and accepted Hitler for his strong government. Economic recovery was the basis of Nazi success, for Hitler realised that maximum support of the people was essential. This was achieved through a fall in unemployment, a rise in profits, control of inflation and a sound currency. Hitler's economic policies 1933–37 successfully achieved a fall in unemployment from the six million of January 1933 to one million in January 1935. ... By 1939 there was a shortage of labour.

Interpretation 2

From Weimar and Nazi Germany, 1918–1939, *by John Child, published in 2016.*

In 1933 the Nazis set up the *Reichs Arbeit Dienst*, or RAD – the National Labour Service. The RAD provided workers for public works, such as repairing roads, planting trees and draining marshes. Apart from giving men work, these projects were also good for Germany as a whole. [...] However, the RAD was not popular. It was organised like an army – workers wore uniforms, lived in camps and did military drill and parades as well as work. Rates of pay were very low and some complained of poor food and working conditions. Some men saw the RAD as service for the Nazi Party or military service rather than normal employment.

The three key questions in the **skills boosts** will help you to explore different options for suggesting a reason why interpretations give different views.

① How do I explain difference based on evidence from the period?

② How do I explain difference based on the historians' emphasis?

③ How do I use the wider historical context to explain difference?

Sources B and C go with the interpretations on page 51.

Source B A graph of unemployment figures using data from The International Labour Review *for the years 1933 to 1939.* The International Labour Review *is a trusted academic journal reporting on industry.*

Source C *From a SOPADE report of 1938. SOPADE was set up by SPD members in exile in Prague from 1933 to 1938, and received reports about life under the Nazis through a secret correspondence system.*

Saxony, April/May 1938: the daily programme of the labour service camp at Beiersfeld/Erzebirge looks like this: 4.45 am get up. 4.50 gymnastics. 5.15 wash, make beds. 5.30 coffee break. 5.50 parade. 6.00 march to building site. Work till 14.30 with 30 minutes' break for breakfast. 15.00 lunch. 15.30–18.00 drill. 18.10–18.45 instruction. 18.45–19.15 cleaning and mending. 19.15 parade. 19.30 announcements. 19.45 supper. 20.00–21.30 sing-song or other leisure activities. 22.00 lights out. The day is thus filled with duties… The wage is 25Pf a day [25 pennies].

(1) Write ✏ a brief description of each of the two sources above. You can use the following to guide you.

| What type of source is it? | What information does it tell us about Germany at the time? |

Writing a brief description of a source in the exam will start you thinking about the information it contains and why it might have been created. This will be helpful in assessing differences between interpretations.

The description for Source B has been started for you:

Source B is a graph of the number of unemployed people in Germany between 1933 and 1939. It shows that

Source C is

(2) These two sources can be connected to Interpretations 1 and 2 on page 51. Tick ✓ the two statements below that provide the most reliable connections.

A | Source C and Interpretation 1 are linked by the Nazis creating a sense of pride in Germany's future. ☐

B | Source B and Interpretation 2 are linked by how the Nazi regime created work for the unemployed. ☐

C | Source B and Interpretation 1 are linked by the fall in unemployment under the Nazi regime. ☐

D | Source C and Interpretation 2 are linked by the way the RAD was organised to be like the army. ☐

There are usually several valid reasons for the different views of the two interpretations. Your explanation and how you support it are key to success with this question.

Employment and living standards in Nazi Germany

This unit uses the theme of employment and living standards in Nazi Germany to build your skills in suggesting a reason why interpretations give different views. If you need to review your knowledge of this theme, work through these pages.

1. Complete this diagram of methods by which the Nazi regime made some unemployment 'invisible' from the statistical record. Some of the methods have been completed already, some have headings but need details, and some are blank and need you to add methods and descriptions. Make sure the descriptions have precise details: look them up if you can't remember them.

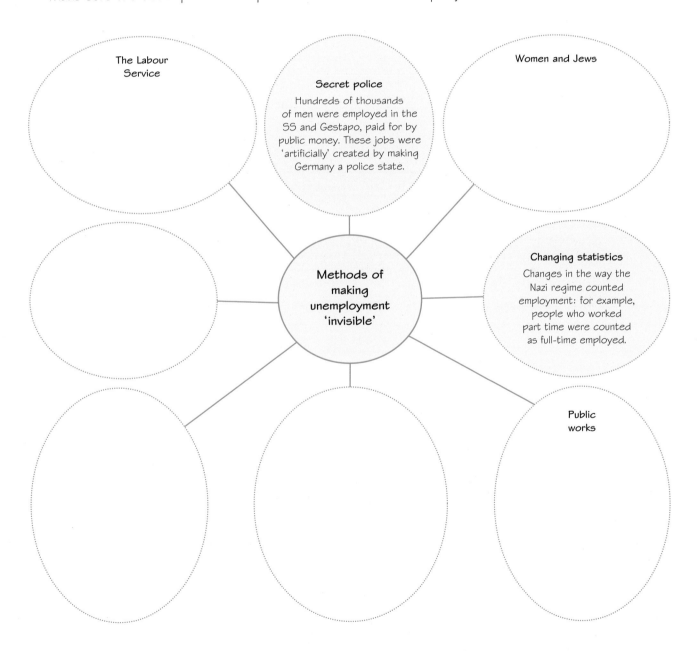

The Labour Service

Secret police
Hundreds of thousands of men were employed in the SS and Gestapo, paid for by public money. These jobs were 'artificially' created by making Germany a police state.

Women and Jews

Methods of making unemployment 'invisible'

Changing statistics
Changes in the way the Nazi regime counted employment: for example, people who worked part time were counted as full-time employed.

Public works

(2) Which of the following statements about changes in the standard of living under the Nazi regime are true and which are false? Tick ✓ to show your decisions.

		true	false
a	In general, the wages of German workers improved under the Nazis.	☐	☐
b	The biggest improvement in wages was between 1936 and 1939.	☐	☐
c	Wages went further because the cost of food decreased in the 1930s.	☐	☐
d	The standard of living for skilled workers went up during the 1930s.	☐	☐
e	The number of families that could afford cars trebled in the 1930s.	☐	☐
f	Low earners/low-skilled workers saw standards of living fall because of high food prices.	☐	☐
g	On average, workers worked less: the average working week fell from about 49 hours in 1933 to about 43 hours in 1939.	☐	☐

(3) Draw ✐ lines to match the following Nazi organisations with their correct descriptions.

A The Labour Front (DAF)

a Provided leisure activities for workers, for example outings and visits to theatre shows. These were subsidised so they were a lot cheaper for members than for others. Also organised saving schemes for the Volkswagen.

B Strength through Joy (KdF)

b Campaigned to get employers to improve facilities for workers, e.g. better canteen facilities. Employers were given tax breaks to encourage them to improve conditions for their workers.

c Replaced trade unions. Set out the rights of workers (e.g. minimum pay levels) and regulated what employers could do. Enforced longer hours and punished workers who disrupted production.

C Beauty of Labour (SdA)

(4) Pick one of the Nazi organisations from **(3)** and identify any positive or negative impacts it had on the standard of living of German workers. ✐

Chosen organisation: ....

Way(s) in which it helped to improve standards of living: ....

....

....

....

....

Limitation(s)/ways in which it did not improve standards of living:...

....

....

....

....

1 How do I explain difference based on evidence from the period?

For this question you have to suggest a reason for the different interpretations, and explain your choice. One approach is to explain a difference based on evidence from the period. This question says, 'You may use Sources B and C to help explain your answer'. Sources B and C provide evidence from the period that may provide help with explaining your suggested reason.

① Look back at the exam-style question, the two interpretations and the two sources on pages 51 and 52. Use them to complete ✎ this table.

	Interpretation 1's view	Interpretation 2's view	Source B's message	Source C's message
Nazi policies to reduce unemployment				

② In the case of these two interpretations and sources, one source supports one interpretation and the other supports the other interpretation. Write ✎ which source (from page 52) supports which interpretation (from page 51):

Interpretation 1 is supported by: ....

Interpretation 2 is supported by: ....

When one of the sources supports one interpretation and the other source supports the different views in the other interpretation, you can use this to help explain your suggested reason.

③ Complete ✎ this student's answer to the exam-style question on page 51, filling in the gaps with the words and phrases in the box below. Use Sources B and C on page 52 to help complete the answer.

unemployment policies	work in a labour camp	evidence	Source B	Source C	military lines

One reason for the difference could be that the interpretations are based on different ....
.... Interpretation 1 could be based on evidence like
.... that shows the overall impact of ....,
while Interpretation 2 could be based on evidence about what it was actually like to ....
...., such as ...., which also suggests
that the work was low paid and organised along strict ....

> Remember that answers for 4-mark questions should be concise and precise. Dealing with these questions efficiently will maximise the time you have available for the higher-mark questions.

② How do I explain difference based on the historians' emphasis?

When the interpretations are focused on different aspects of the topic, we call this having a different **emphasis**. For example, one interpretation might look at a range of different features while the other might focus on one feature in particular. You can use this to explain a difference.

① Look again at Interpretations 1 and 2 on page 51. Tick ✓ the two statements below that best describe each interpretation's emphasis — what it is focusing on.

A | Interpretation 1 deals with a range of features, for example a control on inflation. | ☐

B | Interpretation 1 focuses on how people felt about Hitler's unemployment policies. | ☐

C | Interpretation 1 has a wider emphasis: how Hitler's different economic policies for economic recovery successfully reduced unemployment. | ☐

D | Interpretation 2 deals with a range of features, e.g. types of public works projects. | ☐

E | Interpretation 2 focuses on how the German people felt about Hitler's different unemployment policies. | ☐

F | Interpretation 2 has a narrower emphasis: the RAD and its popularity. | ☐

② Now use your answers to ① to summarise the difference between the two interpretations on page 51. ✏️

One reason for their different views is that they focus on different things about unemployment policies.

While Interpretation 1 ....

....

Interpretation 2 ....

....

③ Use your answers to ① and ② to write ✏️ (on a separate piece of paper) a complete answer to the exam-style question on page 51 that:

- links to the question focus (Nazi policies to reduce unemployment)
- explains what is different about the emphasis of the two interpretations (use your answer to ② here)
- is backed up with precise and concise evidence from both interpretations.

You can follow this template for your answer:

One reason for their different views is that the interpretations focus on different things about [add question focus] while Interpretation 1 [explain its focus], Interpretation 2 [explain its focus]. For example, Interpretation 1 says [select relevant back-up evidence] while Interpretation 2 [select relevant back-up advice].

④ Now go through your answer and cross out ~~cat~~ anything that has over-extended or over-complicated your answer: extra words and phrases that it does not need.

3 How do I use the wider historical context to explain difference?

This skills boost is about yet another approach you can use for explaining a difference between interpretations. If you know the historical context of the topic, then you can explain how interpretations are each providing a piece of the same picture. When an interpretation gives only part of the picture, we call it a **partial** (incomplete) **extract**.

① ⓐ Below are extracts from three student answers. Tick ✓ the one that uses historical context to explain a difference. (The interpretations are not provided here: just read the answers carefully.)

A | *The difference may be because they have given weight to different evidence. Source B provides support for Interpretation 1, which is about opposition to the regime, while Source C gives some support to Interpretation 2, which says there was widespread support for the regime.* | ☐

B | *The difference may be because they are focusing on differing aspects. Interpretation 2 focuses on the extent of support for the regime in different social classes, while the emphasis of Interpretation 1 is on opposition to the regime, especially from youth groups.* | ☐

C | *The difference may be because both interpretations are partial extracts: many social groups did give strong support to the regime, especially the middle classes, while other groups, e.g. workers, were more reluctant to join the Party, for example. Support also changed over time.* | ☐

ⓑ Which of the two remaining extracts is explaining a difference using evidence from the period? Annotate 🖉 it with an E for Evidence.

ⓒ One extract is left. What approach is it using to explain a difference? 🖉

....

② Here is a student's answer to the question on page 51. Which one of the three pieces of relevant historical context below does it use? Tick ✓ your choice.

The interpretations could be different because they are partial extracts. They do not contradict each other. Interpretation 1 concentrates on the way in which the unemployment figures show Nazi unemployment polices to be a success in creating a fall in the numbers unemployed. Interpretation 2 agrees that the RAD provided work, but looks at its quality, saying it was seen as service for the Nazi Party or military service: artificial jobs rather than 'normal' employment.

A | The Nazis used a wide range of methods to 'hide' unemployment figures from the official record. For example, Jews forced out of work were not counted as unemployed and the 'public works' projects created thousands of 'artificial' jobs, using government money. | ☐

B | The Nazis' success in reducing unemployment made them popular because many people had suffered badly in the Depression. Many Germans had also been worried about a Communist revolution in Germany. They were grateful to the Nazis for preventing this. | ☐

C | While the Nazis were successful in reducing unemployment, there is evidence that living standards fell for lower-earning workers. This made it harder to get by than it had been under the Weimar Republic. | ☐

Sample response

Read the answer this student has written to the following exam-style question (Sources B and C are on page 81). Then do the activities that follow it.

Exam-style question

Suggest **one** reason why Interpretations 1 and 2 give different views about support for the Nazi police state.

You may use Sources B and C to help explain your answer.

(4 marks)

Interpretation 1
From The Third Reich in Power, by Richard J. Evans, published in 2006.

Violence and intimidation rarely touched the lives of most ordinary Germans. After 1933 at least, terror was highly selective, concentrating on small and marginal groups [groups on the outside of society] whose persecution not only met with the approval of the vast majority of Germans, but was actually carried out with the co-operation and often voluntary participation at the local level of the broad mass of ordinary German citizens.

Interpretation 2
From Weimar and Nazi Germany 1918–39, by Steve Waugh and John Wright, published in 2016.

A key element in maintaining a Nazi dictatorship was to create a climate of fear – make people too frightened to actively oppose the Nazi state. This was achieved through the establishment of a police state, including a secret police (the Gestapo), the SS, an intelligence agency (the *Sicherheitsdienst*, Security Service), Nazi control of the law courts and the setting up of concentration camps. … If indoctrination [propaganda, education] did not work, then force and terror were used. The Nazis used their own organisations to instil fear into the people.

One reason for the different views could be that the interpretations have given weight to different evidence. Interpretation 1 says that ordinary Germans supported the Nazis' 'terror'. This view is supported by evidence like Source C, which suggests that some Germans thought it was right to 'clean up' the Communists and keep them out of the 'people's community' until 're-education' meant they were no longer a threat. Interpretation 2 says that the purpose of the concentration camps and other elements of the police state was to 'create a climate of fear'. This view is supported by evidence like Source B, which would be terrifying to read ('Social Democratic and Communist officials were dragged from their beds, and beaten, until they collapsed unconscious'), especially for those Germans who had supported other political parties in the past.

(**1**) Circle (A) the approach that this answer has used to suggest a reason.

| A Evidence from the period | B Historians' emphasis | C Historical context |

(**2**) The student has written a good answer that would score the full 4 marks, but they have written more than they need to. Cross out (~~cut~~) the parts of the answer that you think could be cut without losing marks. After your cuts the answer still needs to:

| Suggest a reason for the difference. | Explain the reason. | Link to the question focus. | Support the explanation with relevant details selected from both interpretations. |

Your turn!

Now it's your turn to answer this exam-style question.

① Look again at the question (below). Sources B and C are on page 81. The student on page 58 used evidence from the period to explain the different views. Your task is to write 🖉 your own answer using one of the other two approaches covered in this unit: the historians' emphasis approach or the wider historical context approach. Remember to:

- state the reason you are suggesting: e.g. 'One reason for the difference could be because the interpretations focus on different things about…' (question focus)
- explain the reason
- back up your reason with precisely selected, relevant detail from both interpretations
- keep your answer concise: only write what you need for your 4 marks.

Exam-style question

Suggest **one** reason why Interpretations 1 and 2 give different views about support for the Nazi police state.

You may use Sources B and C to help explain your answer. **(4 marks)**

Interpretation 1 *From The Third Reich in Power, by Richard J. Evans, published in 2006.*

Violence and intimidation rarely touched the lives of most ordinary Germans. After 1933 at least, terror was highly selective, concentrating on small and marginal groups [groups on the outside of society] whose persecution not only met with the approval of the vast majority of Germans, but was actually carried out with the co-operation and often voluntary participation at the local level of the broad mass of ordinary German citizens.

Interpretation 2 *From Weimar and Nazi Germany 1918–39, by Steve Waugh and John Wright, published in 2016.*

A key element in maintaining a Nazi dictatorship was to create a climate of fear – make people too frightened to actively oppose the Nazi state. This was achieved through the establishment of a police state, including a secret police (the Gestapo), the SS, an intelligence agency (the *Sicherheitsdienst*, Security Service), Nazi control of the law courts and the setting up of concentration camps. … If indoctrination [propaganda, education] did not work, then force and terror were used. The Nazis used their own organisations to instil fear into the people.

....

....

....

....

....

....

② Does your answer meet the criteria in the boxes below? Draw 🖉 lines to link the criteria to the relevant content in your answer.

| Suggest a reason for the difference. | Explain the reason. | Link to the question focus. | Support the explanation with relevant details selected from both interpretations. |

Review your skills

Check up

Review your response to the exam-style question on page 59. Tick ✓ the column to show how well you think you have done each of the following.

	Had a go ✓	Nearly there ✓	Got it! ✓
suggested a reason for the difference	☐	☐	☐
explained the reason using evidence, emphasis or the wider historical context	☐	☐	☐
answered concisely, only writing as much as needed for the marks	☐	☐	☐
answered quickly, completing the answer in 6 minutes or less	☐	☐	☐

Look over all of your work in this unit. Note down ✐ the three most important things to remember about how best to suggest a reason why interpretations give different views.

① ....

② ....

③ ....

Need more practice?

If you want to practise another exam-style question, try ✐ the exam-style question below, using the one approach you have not written for it so far (either emphasis or context). The interpretations are on page 59; Sources B and C are on page 81.

Exam-style question

Suggest **one** reason why Interpretations 1 and 2 give different views about support for the Nazi police state.

You may use Sources B and C to help explain your answer.

(4 marks)

How confident do you feel about each of these **skills**? Colour in ✐ the bars.

① How do I explain difference based on evidence from the period?

② How do I explain difference based on the historians' emphasis?

③ How do I use the wider historical context to explain difference?

⑦ Deciding how far you agree with an interpretation

This unit and the next will boost your skills in answering the following type of question successfully. The skills you will build are how to:

- analyse an interpretation to identify the points and evidence that support its view
- use your knowledge of historical context to evaluate interpretations
- use the other interpretation in your evaluation.

Exam-style question

How far do you agree with Interpretation 1 about the reasons for the growth in support for the Nazis in the years 1929 to 1932?

Explain your answer, using both interpretations and your knowledge of the historical context.

(16 marks + 4 marks for spelling, punctuation, grammar and use of specialist terminology)

Interpretation 1
From Years of Weimar, the Third Reich and Post-War Germany, *by David Evans and Jane Jenkins, published in 2008.*

There was a feeling that Germany needed a strong leader and whether people were young or old, male or female, soldier or civilian, worker or peasant, landowner or business man, middle class or aristocrat, they all looked to Hitler as their saviour and redeemer. They staged political rallies with their marching columns of the SA and Sieg Heil shouts (Hail to Victory), their bands, uniforms, banners and flags combined with Hitler's speeches captured the imagination of the masses and gave the illusion of a nation's 'triumph of the will'. Hitler's presence meant that for many, life took on a tremendous new significance.

Interpretation 2
From The Weimar Republic, *by J.W. Hiden, published in 1974.*

Few people are able to think rationally during an economic crisis and they assume that what has happened to them must be somebody's fault – usually the government's. Stable societies can survive economic crises, but there were bound to be very serious problems in Weimar Germany when the economic crisis of 1929 interacted with a political and social crisis. This situation made it possible for opponents of democratic government to become more popular by exploiting the growing resentment against the Republican leaders.

The three key questions in the **skills boosts**, together with the skills in Unit 8, will help you to write an effective answer to this question in the exam.

 1 How do I analyse an interpretation to identify the points and evidence that support its view?

 2 How do I evaluate an interpretation using my knowledge of the context?

3 How do I use the other interpretation in my evaluation?

The final question in the paper asks you to evaluate one interpretation using your own knowledge of the historical context and the other interpretation. It gives you the opportunity to demonstrate your skills of analysis, evaluation and judgement, drawing on your knowledge of the period. The following diagram sets out one way of working through the question.

Analyse Interpretation X to identify the points and evidence that support its view	Analyse first

Analyse Interpretation Y to identify the points and evidence that counter the view in X

Use your analysis points to plan the structure of your answer	Your plan must be organised to review the two views

Use your contextual knowledge to evaluate the points supporting Interpretation X

Do the same to evaluate the points supporting Interpretation Y's counter-argument

Add in any key points missing from the interpretations

Write your answer, remembering to explain and justify your conclusion	Your conclusion must be a substantiated judgement

(1) Draw ✐ lines linking the statements below (about the most successful answers) to the relevant parts of the diagram above.

A | The most successful answers require a precise analysis of the interpretations that indicates how the differences of view are conveyed.

B | The most successful answers require that an overall judgement is justified.

C | The most successful answers require that relevant contextual knowledge is precisely selected to support the evaluation.

D | The most successful answers should review the alternative views.

(2) The statements below are about ways to understand this exam-style question. Tick ✓ the sentences you think are correct. The flow chart above will help you decide.

A | The main aim of this question is to state whether you agree or disagree with the interpretation.

B | The main aim of this question is to evaluate alternative views and make a judgement.

C | The question could ask 'how far you agree' with either Interpretation 1 or Interpretation 2.

D | The question will always be about how far you agree with Interpretation 1.

E | The more historical context you use in your answer, the better your answer.

F | Relevant historical context should be used precisely to support your evaluation.

> The exam paper for the Weimar and Nazi Germany option is structured in such a way that by the time you come to the last question, 'How far do you agree with Interpretation 1 (or 2) about…', you have already identified the main difference between the interpretations and explained a possible reason for the difference. You are already well prepared!

Hitler's appeal: how Hitler became Chancellor

This unit uses the themes of Hitler's appeal and how Hitler became Chancellor to build your skills in deciding how far you agree with an interpretation. If you need to review your knowledge of this theme, work through these pages.

(1) Draw 🖉 lines linking the appeal of the Nazis to these different sections of German society.

A Farmers

a People in this social group had often lost savings and pensions in the Great Depression. Many saw Hitler as a strong leader who could help rebuild Germany and protect their interests. This social group had often been disturbed and upset by social changes under the Weimar Republic, and they agreed with Hitler that traditional German values should be brought back.

B Big business

b Previously this group had tended to support the National Party. But the failure of the Weimar governments to deal with Germany's economic problems, and the rise in support for the KPD, worried this section of society. Hitler promised that the Nazi Party would look after their interests. Nazi finances benefited from large donations by individuals from this group like Benz and Krupps.

C Young people

c In 1928 the Nazis changed their old (1920) policy of confiscating all private land. Now only Jews were to have their land confiscated. The Communists, however, still planned to confiscate all private land, which worried this section of society. They looked to the Nazi Party to protect them from the Communists.

D Working class

d The Nazi Party appealed to many in this section of society because of its dramatic rallies, exciting speeches and Hitler's dedication to changing Germany for the next generation.

e The Nazis tried to appeal to this section of society, which often preferred the KPD, with slogans like 'Work and Bread' – as well as in the name of their Party: the National Socialist German Workers' Party. Members of the Nazi Party from this section of society tended to be unemployed; they were attracted by the Nazis' determination to make the German economy strong again.

E Middle class

(2) Which one of the following correctly illustrates the Nazi Party's results in the Reichstag general elections 1928–32? Tick ✓ your choice.

	May 1928	Sept 1930	July 1932	
A	152 seats	143 seats	133 seats	☐
B	12 seats	107 seats	230 seats	☐
C	54 seats	77 seats	89 seats	☐

(3) Add the following to the timeline below to show the events that led up to Hitler becoming Chancellor.

Presidential elections: Hitler wins 13 million votes	Reichstag elections: Nazis win 230 seats	Von Papen becomes Chancellor
Von Schleicher becomes Chancellor	Presidential elections: Hitler wins 11 million votes	Hitler becomes Chancellor

Chancellor

Chancellor	
Brüning	March 1932
	April 1932
	May 1932
	July 1932
Von Papen	
	December 1932
Von Schleicher	
	January 1933
Hitler	

(4) Use the words below to fill in the gaps in the following text. Two of the words are used twice.

rejected	Schleicher	Papen (×2)	Hindenburg (×2)	Chancellor	July
230	Communist	army	pocket	aeroplane	

Hitler threw all his energy into campaigning in April 1932, even renting an .... to campaign in town after town. The SA broke up .... rallies and there were fights in the streets. The election was won by ...., but Hitler had increased his votes to 13 million, while Thalman, the KPD candidate, lost votes.

In May 1932, Brüning resigned as Chancellor. Von Schleicher, as the representative of an influential group of right-wing landowners, industrialists and army officers, recommended von .... as Chancellor. Then came Reichstag elections in .... 1932. The Nazi Party won a huge number of seats: ...., which was 38% of the Reichstag. Hitler demanded that he be made ....

Hindenburg loathed Hitler and .... this demand. In December 1932, von .... took over as Chancellor, but he was unable to govern because the Nazis would not support him. The Chancellor threatened an .... coup. Faced with this threat, ... agreed to von ....'s proposal – to make Hitler Chancellor and himself vice-Chancellor, because he could control Hitler: he said he had Hitler 'in his ....'.

1 How do I analyse an interpretation to identify the points and evidence that support its view?

The first step is analysis: unpicking the interpretation to identify the different points that make up its view. You can then evaluate these points one by one.

Here's how the student has analysed Interpretation 1 (page 61). This analysis has produced three points to evaluate.

Points from Interpretation 1	Evidence used?	What emphasis?
1 Hitler appealed to many different social groups and both genders	Claim that all Germans felt this way, all classes Long list of supporting groups (12) to show support came from all sections of society	Uses religious language: 'saviour and redeemer' to show appeal Emphasises supporters – no mention of groups who supported other parties
2 Nazi propaganda tactics were important reasons for the growth in support	A long list of tactics in the staged political rallies: marching bands; shouts of 'Sieg Heil'; uniforms, banners and flags; Hitler's speeches	Uses language to suggest the tactics were extremely effective: 'combined... captured the imagination', 'gave the illusion'
3 Hitler had a special quality that attracted people	Felt Germany needed a strong leader People looked to Hitler – he affected their lives	Strong emphasis: 'tremendous new significance' for many

① Now do the same for Interpretation 2 (page 61) using the table below. Write ✐ in the view and at least one more point. One point has been done for you.

- 'Evidence' means the information the historian chooses to include to make a point.
- 'Emphasis' means the way in which the historian gets their point across. Consider: what sort of language do they use to convey their meaning? What have they focused on?

Question focus: reasons for the growth in support for the Nazis, 1929–32		
View given in Interpretation 2:		
Points from Interpretation 2	Evidence used?	What emphasis?
1 Government blamed for people's problems in the economic crisis	People look for someone to blame in a crisis	It was the economic crisis that made the government unpopular

Now you have several points to evaluate for Interpretation 1, using your historical context knowledge. You also have several points to evaluate for Interpretation 2, which is a ready-made counter-argument to Interpretation 1. (Look back at the diagram on page 62.)

2 How do I evaluate an interpretation using my knowledge of the context?

Once you have analysed each interpretation, you can use your knowledge of the historical context to evaluate the strength or weakness of the different views point by point. This is much easier than trying to evaluate the whole interpretation in one go, and it also has two other advantages:

- point-by-point evaluation gives your answer a clear, logical structure
- your evaluation will be precise and relevant because it is focused on one point at a time.

You do not have to use all the points from your analysis: aim to evaluate three points well.

(1) The table below shows three points from the student's analysis of Interpretation 1. Complete the table by adding contextual knowledge (from the boxes below) that supports the point and with contextual knowledge that challenges the point. (Use your own contextual knowledge if you prefer.)

Hitler used an aeroplane in election campaigns in 1930 and 1932.	Although the Nazi Party targeted workers with slogans like 'Work and Bread', more workers preferred the KPD.	Hitler's image was damaged by the street violence of the SA. In July 1932, around 100 were killed in fighting between the SA and KPD.
In the 1930 elections, the Nazis got 60% of the vote in some rural areas.	43% of new Nazi Party members were under 30.	The Nazi vote fell in November 1932, to 196 seats, despite strong speeches and propaganda.

Hitler's speeches were carefully rehearsed to deliver a powerful message and have a powerful emotional impact.

Points from Interpretation 1	Contextual knowledge that supports the point	Contextual knowledge that challenges the point	+~−
Germany needed a strong leader/people saw Hitler in a religious way			
Hitler appealed to many different social groups and both genders			
Hitler's speeches and Nazi propaganda were reasons for the growth in support			

(2) How convincing do you think each point is now that you have evaluated it against your own knowledge?

- If you think contextual knowledge supports a point rather than weakens it, put a plus sign (+) in the final column of the table.
- If contextual knowledge has roughly equal strengthening and weakening effects, put the sign for approximately equal (~) in the final column of the table.
- If contextual knowledge weakens a point rather than strengthens it, put a minus sign (−) in the final column of the table.

3 How do I use the other interpretation in my evaluation?

Since the two interpretations have different views, it makes sense that one interpretation provides a ready-made counter-argument to the other. By evaluating the points from the second interpretation, you can decide with evidence which interpretation you agree with most.

1 **a** The process for evaluating Interpretation 2 is the same as for Interpretation 1. Add the missing contextual knowledge to this table (look it up if you need to). There is only room for two key points here, but you could evaluate more. ✎

b Add your evaluation score (+ ~ −) in the final column. ✎

Points from Interpretation 2	Contextual knowledge that supports the point	Contextual knowledge that challenges the point	+ ~ −
Weimar Germany already had serious problems before the 1929 economic crisis	Reparation payments were still at £50 million a year in 1930. The German economy depended on US loans		
People blamed the Republican leaders for the crisis/for not being able to deal with it		The Nazi vote fell to 196 seats in November 1932, despite the crisis continuing	

At this point you have everything you need to write your answer (look back at the diagram on page 62):

- points from the main interpretation evaluated for strengths and weaknesses
- points from the counter-interpretation evaluated for strengths and weaknesses
- an idea of which interpretation you think is overall stronger or weaker (+ ~ −); this helps you decide how far you agree.

There is one more stage of evaluation that helps you to build up your judgement. It is in the diagram on page 62: What is missing from the interpretations? Use this if neither interpretation has considered something you think is important. This will reduce how far you agree.

2 A student is criticising Interpretations 1 and 2 for not including an important reason for growth in support for the Nazis. Tick ✓ one of the following reasons they could select.

A	The rise in support for the KPD frightened many people into supporting the Nazis, because they wanted to be protected from the threat of a Communist revolution.	☐
B	The Nazis actually got into power because of political intrigues and misjudgements by von Papen and Hindenburg.	☐
C	Many Germans still resented the harsh terms of the Treaty of Versailles.	☐
D	Hitler's appeal cut across classes as an appeal to everyone to build a stronger nation.	☐

Sample response

Here is an extract from a student's answer to the question on page 61, where they evaluate Interpretation 1. (The interpretations are on page 61 as well.)

> Interpretation 1 expresses the view that there was a growth in support for the Nazis after 1929, mainly because of what Hitler and the Nazis did to encourage support, for example Nazi propaganda. This view contrasts with that of Interpretation 2, which sees the economic crisis as being the main reason why people looked to the extreme right and left for solutions.
>
> Interpretation 1 sees support for the Nazis being because Germans saw Hitler as their 'saviour and redeemer'. Sources from the period often refer to Hitler's charisma and appeal, and there is no doubt that many Germans did see him as a religious 'saviour'. Interpretation 1 also carefully selects other ways in which Nazi propaganda 'captured the imagination of the masses', and strongly implies that propaganda was significant in creating an inspiring illusion of Germany's future that convinced 'the masses' to support the Nazis. However, in my view propaganda and Hitler's personal appeal alone cannot explain the rise in support for the Nazis after 1930 (100,000 people joined the party between September and December of 1930). The Nazis' message was based on Mein Kampf, which was published five years earlier, and Hitler's speeches had been powerful emotional performances since at least 1923 (for example, his speeches at his trial). Therefore I do not agree with Interpretation 1's emphasis on Hitler's appeal and Nazi propaganda alone: other factors must have been important in explaining the rapid growth in support for the Nazis after 1929.

1   a   Circle (A) where the student has used material from Interpretation 1 in their evaluation.

    b   Double underline (A) where the student makes a judgement about how far they agree with Interpretation 1.

    c   Underline (A) where the student has used their own knowledge to evaluate interpretation.

2   The next part of the student's answer evaluates Interpretation 2 as a counter-argument to Interpretation 1. It has not used enough material from the interpretation in its evaluation. Improve this paragraph using the statements to the sides. Draw (✏) a line linking each statement to the point at which you would insert it in the answer.

As Interpretation 2 argues, the 'situation made it possible'.

Interpretation 2 makes the point that the crisis was 'bound to' cause serious problems in Weimar Germany.

> I agree with Interpretation 2 that the main reason for the growth in support for the Nazis was the economic crisis following the Wall Street Crash in 1929. People were desperate for a way out of the crisis, and saw the Weimar government as unable to help. Evidence for this includes the fall in votes for SPD: 152 seats in 1928 but 133 in 1932, while the Nazi Party increased their share of the vote from 18% in 1930 to 38% in 1932. I agree that Weimar Germany was very fragile – its economy depended on US loans – but rapid growth in support for the Nazis did not happen before 1929 because before then unemployment was falling (down to 1.3 million in 1928) and wages were rising (up 25% between 1925 and 1928). Therefore I agree that it was the economic situation that allowed Nazi propaganda to have a mass effect.

This allowed opponents of democratic government to exploit this resentment, as Interpretation 2 states.

Interpretation 2's opinion is that when an economic crisis hits, people inevitably blame their own government.

Your turn!

Now it's your turn to use your skills and knowledge in planning an answer to a 'How far do you agree?' exam-style question. Use the skills from this unit to analyse and evaluate the two interpretations for this question. The steps to follow are outlined at the bottom of the page.

Exam-style question

How far do you agree with Interpretation 2 about the reasons for Hitler becoming Chancellor in January 1933?

Explain your answer, using both interpretations and your knowledge of the historical context.

(16 marks + 4 marks for spelling, punctuation, grammar and use of specialist terminology)

Interpretation 1 *From* Understanding the Modern World, *by David Ferriby, Dave Martin and Ben Walsh, published in 2016.*

Through January 1933 Hindenburg and von Papen met secretly with industrialists, army leaders and politicians. And on 30 January, to everyone's great surprise, they offered Hitler the post of Chancellor. Why did they do this? With only a few Nazis in the Cabinet and von Papen as Vice Chancellor, they were confident that they could limit Hitler's influence and resist his extremist demands. The idea was that the policies would be made by the Cabinet, which was filled with conservatives like von Papen. Hitler would be there to get support in the Reichstag for those policies and to control the Communists. So Hitler ended up as Chancellor not because of the will of the German people, but through a behind-the-scenes deal by some German aristocrats.

Interpretation 2 *From Alpha History, a modern history website, by Jennifer Llewellyn, Jim Southey and Steve Thompson, published in 2014.*

Hitler also enjoyed support in other sectors of German society. The NSDAP leader's public image, impressive speech-making and aggressive negotiating had earned him the backing of many wealthy industrialists and business owners. Several notable capitalists had made large political donations to the NSDAP, allowing it to continue its political activities through the worst of the Great Depression. Newspaper mogul Alfred Hugenberg not only provided financial support to Hitler, he also urged his editors to provide the Nazi leader with sympathetic media coverage. Many of these powerful men wrote to Hindenburg, urging him to consider Hitler's appointment as chancellor.

Steps to follow:

1 Break down each interpretation into the individual points that make up its view and show how the author conveys their importance.

2 Review the alternative views to start your answer.

3 Evaluate both interpretations point by point, using your knowledge of the context: does your knowledge support the point or challenge the point?

4 Make sure you use material from both interpretations to support your evaluation.

5 Consider whether both interpretations have missed additional important reason(s).

6 Make judgements on strengths (+) and weaknesses (−) as part of your evaluations.

① Copy and complete ✏ a table like this one in order to help you evaluate and plan an answer.

Points from Interpretation#	Contextual knowledge that supports the point	Contextual knowledge that challenges the point	+ or −

Review your skills

Check up

Review your response to the exam-style question on page 69. Tick ✓ the column to show how well you think you have done each of the following.

	Had a go ✓	Nearly there ✓	Got it! ✓
analysed the points making up each interpretation's view	☐	☐	☐
reviewed the alternative views	☐	☐	☐
evaluated both interpretations against my own historical context knowledge, identifying strengths and weaknesses of the view	☐	☐	☐
made judgements on 'how far I agree' as part of my evaluations	☐	☐	☐

Look over all of your work in this unit. Note down ✐ the three most important things to remember about how best to decide how far you agree with an interpretation.

① ....

② ....

③ ....

Need more practice?

If you want to practise another exam-style question, try ✐ completing your own answer to the following exam-style question, which refers to the interpretations on page 61.

Exam-style question

How far do you agree with Interpretation 1 about the growth in support for the Nazis in the years 1929–32?

Explain your answer, using both interpretations and your knowledge of the historical context.
(16 marks + 4 marks for spelling, punctuation, grammar and use of specialist terminology)

How confident do you feel about each of these **skills**? Colour in ✐ the bars.

1 How do I analyse an interpretation to identify the points and evidence that support its view?
☐ ☐ ☐ ☐

2 How do I evaluate an interpretation using my knowledge of the context?
☐ ☐ ☐ ☐

3 How do I use the other interpretation in my evaluation?
☐ ☐ ☐ ☐

⑧ Conclusions

This unit will help you to enhance your skills in putting together an effective conclusion for the 'How far do you agree?' question, including making your judgement. This judgement needs to be supported by material from the two interpretations combined with your own knowledge. The skills you will build are how to:

- organise the information to help reach a judgement
- plan and construct an effective judgement
- assess the arguments to make a convincing judgement.

This unit focuses on concluding your answer to the 'How far do you agree?' question, which requires you to make your judgement on how far you agree and back up your judgement.

Exam-style question

How far do you agree with Interpretation 2 about the effectiveness of Nazi policies to encourage youth loyalty?

Explain your answer, using both interpretations and your knowledge of the historical context.

(16 marks plus 4 marks for spelling, punctuation, grammar and use of specialist terminology)

Interpretation 1 *From* Youth in the Third Reich, *by D. Peukert, published in 1987.*

The young people of the period 1936–39 had gone through schools that were strongly influenced by National Socialism. Many took being part of the Hitler Youth for granted and saw no alternative to being under its influence. Compared with the benefits of group comradeship [belonging to a group of friends] and leisure activities, they found occasional irritations in the form of brutality and intolerance, drill and demagogy [having to learn about National Socialism], insignificant. And what is more, the Hitler Youth was a rival to traditional authorities of home and school and gave young people a sanctuary that could resist those authorities.

Interpretation 2 *From Alpha History, a modern history website, by Jennifer Llewellyn, Jim Southey and Steve Thompson, published in 2014.*

Many German teenagers shunned the conformity and politicised tone of Nazi youth groups, setting up their own movement called the *Edelweisspiraten* ('Edelweiss Pirates'). The Pirates had chapters [groups] in various German cities, including Berlin, Cologne and Dusseldorf. They dressed flashily, in contrast to drab Nazi uniforms; checked and coloured shirts were commonly worn. The favourite activity of Pirate chapters was ridiculing and antagonising the Hitler Youth and its members. They told dirty jokes about them; sang insulting parodies of Hitler Youth anthems and hymns; taunted and sometimes beat up members. The Pirates also engaged in petty resistance, such as vandalism of Nazi propaganda or buildings.

The three key questions in the **skills boosts** will help you to put together a conclusion that makes a judgement about how far you agree with the interpretation in the question and which is justified by your evaluation.

① How do I organise information to reach a judgement?

② How do I construct an effective conclusion?

③ How do I know what overall judgement to make?

What are the ingredients of a good conclusion?

(1) The following stages of answering a 'How far do you agree?' question have been mixed up. Put them into the right order by numbering 🖉 them 1–4.

For more on planning your response, see Unit 7.

A	Make judgements about how far you agreed with each point, based on whether your evaluation supported them or indicated weaknesses.	☐
B	Analyse the points made by the two interpretations, looking at the information that the two historians selected to convey their view about the question focus and the emphasis they gave to these points.	☐
C	Evaluate the interpretations point by point, using your knowledge of the historical context.	☐
D	Review the main difference between the two interpretations.	☐

Your conclusion makes an overall judgement on how far you agree with the interpretation. This overall judgement is just one of your three essential ingredients for a good, clear conclusion:

- your overall judgement on how far you agree
- evidence to back up your judgement from the two interpretations
- evidence to back up your judgement from your own knowledge.

Develop your judgement directly from your evaluation of both interpretations. Do not introduce new ingredients in the conclusion!

There is no 'right' answer to a 'How far do you agree?' question. If one student's answer agrees with Interpretation 1 and another backs Interpretation 2, they can both get exactly the same marks. What is important is the way the argument is made.

(2) Read the following conclusion to the question on page 71 and identify where the three essential ingredients of a good conclusion are shown.

(a) Highlight 🖉 text where the overall judgement is given.

(b) Underline (A) where the student uses evidence from Interpretation 1 (on page 71) to back up their judgement.

(c) Double underline (A) where the student uses evidence from Interpretation 2 (on page 71) to back up their judgement.

(d) Circle (A) where the student uses evidence from their own knowledge to back up their judgement.

I agree more with Interpretation 1 than Interpretation 2 about how effective Nazi policies were at encouraging youth loyalty. Interpretation 1 is more convincing about most young people going along with Nazi youth organisations, rather than resisting them: even if they did dislike the Hitler Youth lessons and military drill, they did like being together as a group, being able to do sporting activities and being protected from having to do everything their parents and teachers said. Although Edelweiss Pirate groups were set up by young people who really hated the 'conformity and politicised tone' of Nazi youth groups, there were only around 2,000 Edelweiss Pirates by 1939, compared with 8 million Hitler Youth members. Not all of these Hitler Youth members were loyal to the Nazi Party: many probably would rather not have had to go, but I agree with Interpretation 1 that the Nazis were effective in making organisations like the Hitler Youth something that young people took for granted rather than something they thought about resisting.

Nazi policies towards the young

This unit uses the theme of Nazi policies towards the young to build your skills in writing conclusions. If you need to review your knowledge of this theme, work through these pages.

1 The statements below are about the aims of Nazi policies towards the young. Only one statement in each pair is true. Tick ✓ the statement in each pair that correctly describes a Nazi aim.

A | All girls were brought up to be strong and healthy, so they could become strong and healthy workers for the German government. | ☐

B | All girls were brought up to be strong and healthy, so they could become healthy, fertile mothers and strong, effective wives. | ☐

C | All boys were brought up to be strong and healthy, so they could be strong and healthy workers and effective soldiers in Germany's armed forces. | ☐

D | All boys were brought up to be strong and healthy so they could be good husbands and bring up lots of healthy German children. | ☐

E | Parents encouraged German children to become Nazi Party members when they were old enough. | ☐

F | Nazi policies made sure that German children grew up believing in Nazi aims and policies in case their parents were not Nazi supporters. | ☐

G | Since German children were the future of the Thousand Year Reich, they were brought up to be proud Germans who supported a strong, independent Germany. | ☐

H | Since German children were the future of the Thousand Year Reich, they were brought up to recognise the weaknesses of the German nation that had to be repaired. | ☐

2 Draw ✏ lines linking the following Nazi youth groups to the gender and age groups they were for.

A Young Maidens	a 14–18-year-old boys/young men
B German Young People	b 14–21-year-old girls/young women
C Hitler Youth	c 6–10-year-old boys
D League of German Maidens	d 10–14-year-old boys
E Little Fellows	e 10–14-year-old girls

3 Use the words below to fill in (✎) the gaps in the following text about the Hitler Youth.

| lessons | political | report | courses | oath | parents | Jews | Nazi Party |

> Although it was designed to train its members physically and militarily, the Hitler Youth was
>
> primarily a .... group that aimed to influence boys and young men to become ....
>
> members. There were four main ways in which this was done. All Hitler Youth members had to
>
> swear an .... of loyalty to the Führer. Members were required to go on residential
>
> .... about Nazi ideas. Every year group of the Hitler Youth had a course of ....
>
> to study, which included lessons on 'German heroes' and 'The evil of the ....'. And Hitler
>
> Youth members were encouraged to .... anyone they observed who was not being loyal
>
> to the Nazis, even if this meant reporting their own ....

4 Answer the following questions about Nazi education policies. Write (✎) your answer in the space provided after each question.

a After 1933, all teachers had to join which Nazi organisation?

> The Nazi Teachers ....
>
> ....

b State an additional two ways in which teachers were expected to promote Nazi ideas and beliefs (one has been completed for you).

> Teachers taught students how to do the Hitler salute. ....
>
> ....
>
> ....

5 Read the following source, then answer the question that follows.

Source A *From a report to the Gestapo by the Düsseldorf branch of the Nazi Party. This report was made in 1943.*

> RE: Edelweiss Pirates question… These youngsters, aged between 12 and 17, hang around into the late evening, with musical instruments and young females. Since this riff-raff is to a large extent outside the Hitler Youth and adopts a hostile attitude towards it, they are a danger to other young people… There is a suspicion that it is these youths who have been inscribing the walls of the subway on the *Altenbergstrasse* [Altenberg Street] with the slogans 'Down with Hitler'… 'Down with Nazi brutality', etc.

Give (✎) two things you can infer from Source A about Nazi youth policies.

....

....

....

....

....

....

....

How do I organise information to reach a judgement?

You can use your evaluation points to reach a judgement. After you have evaluated your points from the first interpretation, make a mini-judgement. Do the same after you have evaluated the counter-argument interpretation. Then combine the mini-judgements for the overall judgement.

Here is what one student did for their evaluation of Interpretation 1 on page 71.

Points from Interpretation 1	Contextual knowledge that supports the point	Contextual knowledge that challenges the point	+~-	
By 1939 young people had only known the Nazi education system	11-year-olds in 1939 would have been 5 in 1933: they would have had all-Nazi education	Those aged 16 and over in 1939 would have had a non-Nazi primary education	+	Mini-judgement = overall, contextual knowledge supports this point
Many young people took the Hitler Youth for granted and didn't think about alternatives	From 1936 there were no alternatives to Nazi youth groups for sports; 1933: other youth groups were banned	Edelweiss Pirates: perhaps 2,000 – compared with 8 million Hitler Youth?	+	Mini-judgement = overall, contextual knowledge challenges this point
The Hitler Youth had more advantages than disadvantages	Sources provide evidence that young people enjoyed feeling part of a group	By 1938, attendance at youth meetings was so poor (25%) that attendance was made compulsory	-	

(1) How far would you say the student agrees with Interpretation 1? Tick ✓ your choice.

Strongly agree ☐ Generally agree ☐ Generally disagree ☐ Strongly disagree ☐

This is how the student evaluates the strengths and weaknesses of Interpretation 1.

> Interpretation 1 asserts that by 1939 young people would have only known the Nazi education system: this would be true for children, but 16- and 17-year-olds would have been educated under the Weimar system. Interpretation 1 argues this to set up their second point, that many young people took the Hitler Youth for granted because they had never known an alternative. It is true that from 1936 there were no alternative ways to access sports activities, and other youth groups, such as Church groups, had been banned since 1933. To strengthen their view that most young people went along with Nazi youth organisations, Interpretation 1 gives two main advantages (togetherness and leisure activities) that overcame the 'occasional' disadvantages of things like military drill. However, by 1938 only a quarter of young people were attending the youth organisations, which was why the Nazis made attendance compulsory. This suggests that by 1938 there were not as many advantages.

(2) On a separate piece of paper, write ✏ a mini-judgement for this answer extract to say **how far the student agrees** with Interpretation 1's view of the effectiveness of Nazi policies to encourage youth loyalty. Ensure your mini-judgement is linked to the question focus.

② How do I construct an effective conclusion?

You should aim to make your conclusion clear and logically organised so the examiner can easily understand how far you agree and the reasons for your judgement.

1 Whether you agree or disagree with the interpretation. How far you agree…	→	2 Reasons why you agree and reasons why you disagree.	→	3 Final sentence that links back to the question focus.

The most successful answers will follow the approach shown in the flow diagram.

① ⓐ Tick ✓ the pieces of advice below that you agree would enhance your conclusion. Put a cross ✗ by any pieces of advice that you disagree with.

A | Indicate how far you agree rather than a straight 'I agree' or 'I disagree'. | ☐

B | Review the views made by both interpretations to remind readers what each is about. | ☐

C | Include only the strengths of the interpretation you agree with and only the limitations of the one you do not agree with. | ☐

D | Weigh up the strengths and limitations of both interpretations to reach an overall judgement. | ☐

E | State which factor you consider is the most important cause and explain why. | ☐

F | Summarise every evaluation point that you made in your answer. | ☐

G | Select your justification evidence precisely and concisely to make a convincing case. | ☐

H | Link your judgement to the question focus. | ☐

ⓑ What order would you put your ticked choices in to structure an effective conclusion? Write ✎ the letters of your choices here, in the order you would include them.

....

② The following statements are from one student's conclusion. See if you can match any of the statements to the pieces of advice you ticked in ①. Write ✎ the letters in the spaces.

I agree with aspects of both interpretations, although in my view Interpretation 1 is strongest.	
There is evidence that supports Interpretation 2's point that…	
However, Interpretation 2 fails to account for…	
Interpretation 1 is not convincing when it argues that…	
But the strength of Interpretation 1's main view is clearly confirmed by…	
And I find the following to be the most convincing argument in favour of Interpretation 1…	
Therefore, in terms of the question focus, my overall judgement is that…	

3 How do I know what overall judgement to make?

There is no 'right' judgement for the 'How far do you agree?' question. What is needed is an overall judgement that is effectively justified by the evaluation work you have done in the main part of the answer. Your overall judgement can then be built from your evaluation mini-judgements.

① Study these two mini-judgements from a student's answer to the question on page 71.

Mini-judgement: Interpretation 1	Mini-judgement: Interpretation 2
I generally agree with Interpretation 1's view that most young people went along with the Hitler Youth, because there were not really any alternatives for young people after 1933, when the Nazis closed down Church youth groups. However, by 1938 three-quarters of young people were failing to attend Nazi youth organisations. This challenges Interpretation 1's view that the Nazis were successful in ensuring that young people accepted being part of Nazi youth organisations.	Interpretation 2's view that many German teenagers rejected the Hitler Youth is not convincing because there were only around 2,000 Edelweiss Pirates compared with 8 million Hitler Youth members by 1939. Some teenagers definitely did reject the Nazis' attempt to make them into loyal Nazis, but their numbers seem too low for this to be something you can say was true for most young people in Germany.

ⓐ Decide how far the student agrees with each interpretation. Draw ✎ and label two arrows on the continuum line to show this.

Strongly
agree

Strongly
disagree

ⓑ On a separate piece of paper, explain ✎ why the student agrees/disagrees with the interpretations.

Your overall judgement needs to:
- say how far you agree with the interpretation in its view of the question focus
- be 'substantiated': it needs to be backed up by evidence from your evaluation, some from the interpretations and some from your own knowledge.

② Complete ✎ this overall judgement for the student.

I strongly disagree with Interpretation 2's view that [link view to question focus] ....

....

My main reason for this is [summarise evidence why not] ....

....

I find Interpretation 1's view generally more convincing because [summarise evidence why] ....

....

In conclusion, Nazi policies to encourage youth loyalty were [link Interpretation 1's view to question focus]

....

Sample response

Knowing how to write an effective conclusion is very important in convincing the reader of the arguments you presented. Remember, the three essential ingredients of a conclusion for this type of exam question are:

1 your overall judgement on how far you agree

2 evidence to back up your judgement from the two interpretations

3 evidence to back up your judgement from your own knowledge.

A student has written the following conclusion to the question on page 71.

Exam-style question

> How far do you agree with Interpretation 2 about the effectiveness of Nazi policies to encourage youth loyalty?

I strongly agree with Interpretation 2's view that Nazi policies to encourage youth loyalty failed. Interpretation 2 uses the Edelweiss Pirates as evidence of the way many German teenagers completely rejected Nazi youth organisations, especially the constant political pressure on Hitler Youth members to swear loyalty to the Nazis and to learn to think and act in Nazi ways. One criticism of Interpretation 2 is that there were only ever small numbers of Edelweiss Pirates, 2,000 in total, but there are good reasons to think that many more German teens were very reluctant to go to Nazi youth organisations. In 1938 attendance had to be made compulsory, because only 25% of young people were attending Nazi youth organisations. This is also why I only partly agree with Interpretation 1, which argues that young people went along with Nazi youth organisations because they didn't know anything different. While I agree that many teens would have enjoyed the leisure activities, I am convinced that the low attendance figures prove that Nazi policies to encourage youth loyalty were why the youth organisations became unpopular, showing that the policy failed.

1 The student above strongly agrees with Interpretation 2. Are they right? Tick ✓ your choice.

A | This student is right to strongly agree with Interpretation 2. | ☐

B | This student is wrong to strongly agree with Interpretation 2. | ☐

C | There is no 'right' answer, what is important is how you substantiate your judgement. | ☐

2 **a** Highlight 🖊 in one colour where the student makes their overall judgement.

b Underline Ⓐ where the student substantiates (backs up) their overall judgement using material from Interpretation 2.

c Double underline Ⓐ where the student substantiates their overall judgement using material from Interpretation 1.

d Circle Ⓐ where the student substantiates their overall judgement using their own knowledge.

e Highlight 🖊 in a second colour where the student links their overall judgement to the question focus.

Your turn!

Now it's your turn to try to answer an exam-style question.

(1) Write ✏️ the whole answer on a separate piece of paper using the skills boosts from Unit 7, then build your conclusion from your evaluation, using the skills on making and justifying an overall judgement from this unit.

Exam-style question

How far do you agree with Interpretation 1 about the effectiveness of Nazi control of teaching?

Explain your answer, using both interpretations and your knowledge of the historical context.

(16 marks plus 4 marks for spelling, punctuation, grammar and use of specialist terminology)

Interpretation 1 From Germany 1918–1945, by Steve Waugh, published in 2013.

The Nazis used education as a method of indoctrinating the young with Nazi ideas, that is, teaching them to accept their views. This was achieved by controlling all aspects of education.

It became compulsory for teachers to join the Nazi Party and swear an oath of loyalty. Many teachers attended teachers' camps, which concentrated on how to indoctrinate the young and on physical training. Nearly all teachers joined the Nazi Teachers' Association.

Interpretation 2 From The Third Reich in Power, by Richard J. Evans, published in 2006.

Violence and intimidation rarely touched the lives of most ordinary Germans. After 1933 at least, terror was highly selective, concentrating on small and marginal groups [groups on the outside of society] whose persecution not only met with the approval of the vast majority of Germans, but was actually carried out with the co-operation and often voluntary participation at the local level of the broad mass of ordinary German citizens.

Remember, for the 'How far do you agree?' question you need to:

1 Analyse both interpretations to identify the points for your evaluation.
2 Evaluate one interpretation using your knowledge of the historical context.
3 Evaluate the counter-argument interpretation in the same way.
4 Use your evaluation strengths and limitations to reach judgements about each interpretation.
5 Construct an effective conclusion that contains the three essential ingredients.
6 Link how far you agree back to the question focus.

Review your skills

Check up

Review your response to the exam-style question on page 79. Tick ✓ the column to show how well you think you have done each of the following.

	Had a go ✓	Nearly there ✓	Got it! ✓
analysed both interpretations to identify points for evaluation	☐	☐	☐
evaluated each interpretation using knowledge of the historical context	☐	☐	☐
made an overall judgement that was substantiated	☐	☐	☐
linked the judgement back to the question focus	☐	☐	☐

Look over all of your work in this unit. Note down ✎ the three most important things to remember about how best to write an effective conclusion.

① ....

② ....

③ ....

Need more practice?

If you want to practise another exam-style question, try ✎ the exam-style question below.
The interpretations you need to complete this answer are on pages 82 and 83.

Exam-style question

How far do you agree with Interpretation 2 about reactions to the Nazis' policies on unemployment?

Explain your answer, using both interpretations and your knowledge of the historical context.

(16 marks plus 4 marks for spelling, punctuation, grammar and use of specialist terminology)

How confident do you feel about each of these **skills**? Colour in ✎ the bars.

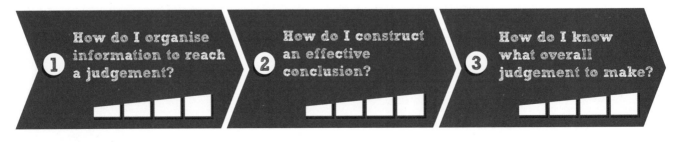

1 How do I organise information to reach a judgement?

2 How do I construct an effective conclusion?

3 How do I know what overall judgement to make?

More practice texts

This source is used for the exam-style question on page 10.

Source A *From a speech to representatives of the press (newspaper and radio) by Goebbels on 15 March 1933 about the Ministry for Popular Enlightenment and Propaganda.*

We cannot be satisfied with just telling the people what we want and enlightening [explaining to] them as to how we are doing it. We must replace this enlightenment with an active government propaganda that aims at winning people over. It is not enough to reconcile people more or less to our regime, to move them towards a position of neutrality towards us, we would rather work on people until they are addicted to us.

These sources are used for the exam-style question on page 30.

Source B *Part of a letter written by a Freikorps soldier to his family in April 1920.*

Our battalion has two deaths, the Reds [Communists] 200–300. Anyone who falls into our hands gets the rifle butt and then is finished off with a bullet… We even shot ten Red… nurses on sight because they were carrying pistols. We shot those little women with pleasure – how they cried and pleaded with us to save their lives. No chance! Anyone with a gun is our enemy.

Source C *Part of a letter written to a Social Democratic Party newspaper in 1919.*

Our government does little to ensure the fair distribution of food. … There is bacon in the windows [of butchers' shops] but the workers cannot afford to buy it … Every day 800 people die of starvation… and the children who die are not the children of the rich. For how long will such injustice be allowed to go on? … The time might not be too distant when a general strike will brush away this government.

These sources are used for the exam-style questions on page 37 and page 58.

Source B *From a pamphlet written and distributed by a group of banned Communists in April 1933.*

Listen! Read! Pass it on! Hitler's Crimes!
In Berlin alone thousands of Social Democratic and Communist officials were dragged from their beds at night… and led away to SA barracks. There they were worked over with boot and whip, beaten with steel rods and rubber truncheons until they collapsed unconscious and blood spurted under their skin. Many were forced to drink castor oil or had urine directed into their mouths; others had their bones broken. Working-class officials were tortured to death by these and similar methods of torture.

Source C *From private letters written in March and April 1933 by Elisabeth Gebensleben, a 49-year-old Nazi supporter and wife of her town's deputy mayor, to her friend Irmgard Brester.*

The ruthless intervention of the nationalist [Nazi] government might appear strange to some people, but first we have to systematically clean up. The Communists [KPD] have to disappear, and Marxists too [the Social Democrats]. All those people who suddenly want to become National Socialists should not be welcome… until they have served a three-year probationary period in the concentration camps.

These sources are used for the exam-style question on page 40.

These sources are used for the exam-style question on page 40.

Source B | *From a letter by 'Hans J.' sent to the Social Democratic Party headquarters in Hanover on 9 March 1933. Hans J. sent this letter to explain his resignation from the SDP.*

As a civil servant [a government employee] I have to make a choice. On the one hand, I see how my employer, the Reich government, tends not to tolerate its employees belonging to anti-Government associations. On the other hand, there is my loyalty to the Social Democratic Party. Unfortunately, I see no solution but my resignation. The existence of my family is at stake. If I do end up being made unemployed, which in my experience can be very, very hard, then at least I won't feel that I did not do everything in the interests of my wife and child.

Source C | *From the diary of Victor Klemperer, a Jewish university lecturer living in Germany in 1933. This extract is from 14 November 1933, two days after elections to the Reichstag.*

The results were published yesterday: 93 per cent vote for Hitler! 40.5 million 'Yes', 2 million 'No'… Even in the concentration camps most had voted 'Yes'. But that is undoubtedly either because the results were faked or because people were forced to vote for the Nazis. … Gusto Wieghardt told me recently that an advertising brochure for some electrical goods or other had been sent to her. In the middle of the advertising text there had been a Communist article. But what good do such pinpricks do? Less than none. Because all Germany prefers Hitler to the Communists.

These interpretations are used for the exam-style question on page 50.

Interpretation 1 | *From Weimar Germany, by John R.P. McKenzie, published in 1971.*

One of the major problems with the Constitution was that it did not anticipate the need for the Republic to deal with anti-democratic threats. A model 'free' Constitution, it failed to realise that democracy can only flourish in a society which wishes to be democratic. Instead, the Constitution gave extremists the right to undermine democratic government through the voting system. This contributed to the downfall of the Republic.

Interpretation 2 | *From Second Reich to Third Reich: Germany 1918–1945, by Geoff Layton, published in 2008.*

The new constitution was a great improvement upon the previous undemocratic constitution of Imperial Germany and a very large majority of Germans voted in favour of it. The Weimar Republic had other more serious problems than just the Constitution, such as the Treaty of Versailles and its socio-economic problems. …

It seems unrealistic to imagine that any piece of paper could have resolved all Germany's problems after 1918. The Weimar Constitution had weaknesses, but it was not fatally flawed – there were many more serious and fundamental problems within the Weimar Republic.

This interpretation and Interpretation 2 overleaf are used for the exam-style question on page 80.

Interpretation 1 | *From Years of Weimar and the Third Reich, by David Evans and Jane Jenkins, published in 1999.*

Many people came to feel a sense of pride in Germany's future and accepted Hitler for his strong government. Economic recovery was the basis of Nazi success, for Hitler realised that maximum support of the people was essential. This was achieved through a fall in unemployment, a rise in profits, control of inflation and a sound currency. Hitler's economic policies 1933–37 successfully achieved a fall in unemployment from the six million of January 1933 to one million in January 1935. … By 1939 there was a shortage of labour.

From Weimar and Nazi Germany, 1918–1939, *by John Child, published in 2016.*

In 1933 the Nazis set up the *Reichs Arbeit Dienst*, or RAD – the National Labour Service. The RAD provided workers for public works, such as repairing roads, planting trees and draining marshes. Apart from giving men work, these projects were also good for Germany as a whole. … However, the RAD was not popular. It was organised like an army – workers wore uniforms, lived in camps and did military drill and parades as well as work. Rates of pay were very low and some complained of poor food and working conditions. Some men saw the RAD as service for the Nazi Party or military service rather than normal employment.

Answers

Unit 1

Page 2

(1) D

(2) (a) C; (b) B; (c) A

Page 3

(1) A, C, D and E

(2) A = c; B = e; C = f; D = d; E = a; F = b

Page 4

(4)

Extremist left wing		Moderate parties				Extremist right wing	
KPD	SPD	DDP	ZP	DVP	DNVP	NSDAP
Communist Party	Social Democrats	Democrats	Centre Party	People's Party	National Party	Nazi Party
Opposed Weimar Republic	Supported Weimar Republic	Supported Weimar Republic	Supported Weimar Republic	Sometimes supported Republic	Grudgingly accepted Republic	Opposed Weimar Republic

(5) 1: C, 2: E, 3: B.

(6) (a) False (b) False (c) True (d) True (e) False

Page 5

(1) C

(2) A: This inference is not supported by the source – it is correct information about the causes of hyperinflation, but the inference has to be something taken from the source itself.
B: The answer makes a valid inference but it also makes two inferences and includes unnecessary detail that takes up exam time but does not score any more marks.

Page 6

(1) C

(2) The answer has not made an inference that is directly supported by the source.

(3) (a) D
(b) D is a valid inference because it is supported directly by the source's content: a vampire representing France is victimising a woman representing Germany. It is linked to the question focus by: saying that the French prime minister 'was blamed for the harshness of the Treaty to Germany' – that is, reactions in Germany were that France was to blame.

Page 7

(1) (a) Source A describes how unemployed people 'stood around by the thousands and shook their fists at the profiteers'.
(b) For example, Source A says that profiteers and foreigners were able to buy 'whole rows of streets like a box of matches'.

(2) (a) This is suggested in Source A by the evil vampire, representing France, sucking blood out of the figure representing Germany.

(3) (a) The idea of the November Criminals weakened the Weimar Republic because it was the idea that the leaders of the Weimar Republic who had signed the Treaty of Versailles in Germany had betrayed Germany by accepting such harsh terms.

(b) The idea of the 'Diktat' weakened the Weimar Republic because it was the idea that Germany had not been allowed any role in the Versailles negotiations, which made the Treaty unfair, which meant the Weimar Republic was wrong to do what the Treaty said, e.g. pay reparations.

(b) This is shown in Source A by Germany being represented as a woman lying helpless on a bed while being attacked by the vampire President of France.

(3) For example:

~~Because of the hyperinflation, everyday life became very difficult for most people because~~ money stopped having any real value in 1923: ~~people needed millions of marks just to pay for really ordinary things.~~ Source A shows this with bundles of banknotes ~~in the photo being~~ used as toys ~~by children, which would never usually have happened because money used to be really valuable and if the children had lost even one banknote or damaged even one banknote it would have been a waste.~~

~~Hyperinflation also meant~~ there were very large numbers of banknotes in circulation, ~~which meant people had to find ways of transporting all the cash they needed, making life difficult especially since the money had to be spent quickly before it lost its value.~~ Source A shows ~~this because is suggests~~ that the one family ~~represented by the children in the photo~~ had ~~got so much money that the children have~~ enough to make a large pyramid ~~out of it, with bundles of banknotes to spare.~~

Page 8

(1) The student has done a good job and did both things for each point on the checklist.

(2) For example:
Source A suggests the Nazis were worried about whether ordinary people supported them.
For example, Ley's question 'Haven't you got any Nazis at all?'
It was sensible to say you supported the Nazis, even if you didn't.
The joke's punchline is that all these non-Nazis **say** they are Nazis.

(3) Since the answer would get 4 marks out of 4, advice should be to save time (at least 4 minutes) by only giving as much as the question requires – two valid inferences with two precisely selected supporting details.

Page 9

(1) For example:

What I can infer: The source suggests that the Strength Through Joy trips were succeeding in raising living standards for ordinary German workers.

Details in the source that tell me this: Source A says that people from 'simple backgrounds' could afford to take 'lovely holidays' because the scheme made them cheap enough: 60 marks covered all expenses where usually the travel alone would have cost 100 marks.

What I can infer: The source shows that even opponents of the Nazis recognised that some of their policies were genuinely popular with German people.

Details in the source that tell me this: The source was written for SOPADE, exiled opponents of the Nazis, but it still says that the scheme is 'stimulating our tourist trade considerably'.

Unit 2
Page 12

(1) The stimulus points are covered in the first two causes of the plan.

(2) The student has brought in their own information in the third cause of the plan.

(3) **Tick:** A, B, C and D

(4) It is a strong plan; a possible weakness is that the Dawes Plan and the Young Plan both involved reducing reparation payments, so to make sure that three **different** causes are explained, the student will need to be careful to identify other causes arising from the two plans.

Page 13

(1) A = e; B = c; C = a; D = b; E = d

(2)

Policy	What the policy did	Impact on Germany
The Locarno Pact (1925)	A treaty between Germany, Britain, France, Italy and Belgium that fixed borders and demilitarised the Rhineland, promoting peace, and started discussions for Germany to join the League of Nations.	Germany had lost importance internationally and the Locarno Pact treated Germany as an equal again, increasing confidence. The threat of war starting again also lessened.\n\nHowever, extremist political parties criticised the Locarno Pact for agreeing to the borders set out by the hated Treaty of Versailles.
Joining the League of Nations (1926)	Germany was accepted into the League of Nations and gained a place on the League of Nations Council.	Germany had been excluded from the League of Nations: being included boosted Germany's prestige. Stresemann felt membership would make it easier for Germany to improve its position in future treaties. However, extremist parties were unhappy because the League of Nations was associated with the Treaty of Versailles.
The Kellogg-Briand Pact (1928)	A pact in 1928 between 15 countries plus Germany, later signed by over 60 nations, that they would not use war to achieve foreign-policy aims.	Germany was now established as an equal party with other powerful countries, which boosted its confidence as a country and helped to increase support for the Weimar government. However, because it did not restore any of Germany's losses from the Treaty of Versailles, extremist parties opposed it.

Page 14

(3) Students should add in this order: the way women had worked for the war effort; who led the Weimar government in 1918; 10% of Reichstag members were women; of the Weimar Constitution guaranteed important rights for women; women were paid around one third less than men; this figure had halved by 1925; These 'new women' expressed their independence; short haircuts, more make-up; and going out unaccompanied by men.

(4) A and C are true. B and D are false.

Page 15

(1) Student's own response.

(2) Sample plan:

Because: Better discussions re reparations

The Locarno Pact

Back up: 1925, France Belgium, Britain, Italy

Because: helped set up Young Plan

Kellogg-Briand Pact

Back up: August 1928, 62 countries

Reasons why Stresemann's foreign policy helped WR's recovery

Because: More confidence in Stresemann

League of Nations

Back up: Sept 1926

Because: no real impact on WR recovery?

Treaty of Berlin

Back up: April 1926, with USSR

Page 16

(1) (The Rentenmark) was a reason for/helped the economic recovery in the Weimar Republic because

(2) Votes for women (November 1918) improved the position of women in German society because not having the vote made women seem less important than men. As voters, women could influence Germany's politics, and as politicians, women could make sure that women's interests were represented.

Women in the workplace improved the position of women in German society because women gained financial independence: they no longer had to rely on men and could make their own decisions about their lives. Progress was greatest in government jobs: in many jobs women were paid less than men and were expected to stop work when they married.

Article 109 of the Weimar Constitution improved the position of women in German society because it strengthened their rights to equality in the workplace (equal pay), to equality in the marriage partnership and their right to enter any profession on an equal basis with men. These improvements were greatest in government jobs, such as health care and education. Outside government jobs, the private sector was slow to allow women their rights.

Page 17

(1) **a** and **b** The Unemployment Insurance Act (1927) helped standards of living improve between 1923 and 1929 because it provided unemployment and sickness benefit to German workers. In 1924, over 4% of the total

workforce was unemployed. The Unemployment Insurance Act charged 16.4 million workers 3% of their wages: this money was used to provide an average of 60 marks per week in benefits for those out of work or unable to work, which substantially improved standards of living for those receiving these payments.

2. For example:

Building new houses: In 1923, there was a shortage of 1 million homes. This contributed to lower living standards because it meant people were often living in cramped and overcrowded conditions. In 1925, a 15% rent tax was introduced. This funded new building associations: 2 million new homes were built between 1924 and 1931, which directly tackled the problems of overcrowding and meant many more people had better places to live. State spending on housing was 33% higher in 1929 compared with 1913. Homelessness had reduced by 60% by 1928, which meant a big improvement in standards of living for those who had been living on the streets or without proper housing.

Pensions for war veterans: War veterans, especially those who had been wounded and disabled in the war, often struggled to find work and had to endure poor living conditions. Pensions were paid throughout the 1920s to 750,000 war veterans, 400,000 war widows and 200,000 parents of dead servicemen. This improved living standards not only for veterans who had not been able to find work, but also for families left without a husband or son because of the war, who also often struggled to earn enough to live on.

Page 18

1. They worked and were financially independent. They wore make-up and had short hair, which were not traditional. They also smoked and drank, and this was not accepted behaviour.; like the paintings of Otto Dix, the Bauhaus school of design and Fritz Lang's films; unemployment never dipped below 1.3 million in Weimar Germany; Article 109; By 1925, only 36% of women were in work, the same as before the war

2. In the first paragraph, the student does not develop the point about 'not accepted behaviour': the answer should explain why increased independence for women was linked by some to women having fewer babies and higher rates of divorce, contrasted with the traditional belief that women should be wives and mothers, so increasing social tension between new women and traditional Germans.

   In the second paragraph, the student does not link back to the question enough. The reason why cultural experimentation increased social tensions needs to be developed. For example, criticism of government funding for cultural experimentation came from Communists because the money could have been used to support unemployed people and people living in poverty. Conservatives, however, hated the way cultural experimentation explored dark areas of Germany's war experiences and pointed out the squalid conditions many Germans were now living in: conservatives thought the purpose of art was to inspire and celebrate the greatness of Germany as a nation and people.

3. The answer does include three explanations, at least one of which is the student's own knowledge. Explanation 1 needs to be developed more to link to the question focus. Explanation 2 is not really linked to the question focus at all. The supporting detail is accurate and relevant in explanation 3 in particular, but more supporting detail would have improved explanations 1 and 2 further.

4. Student's own response.

Page 19

1. and 2. Student's own response.

Unit 3
Page 22

1. **Nature:** a photograph/newspaper photograph.

   Origin: an unknown photographer. The source information does not provide any extra help with this, making origin more difficult to use in judging usefulness in this case.

   Purpose: to record the defendants in the trial. Since the men are posed and dressed impressively, the purpose could also be inferred to show the German public that the defendants were serious, senior men and to remind the public of Ludendorff's war hero status.

Page 23

1. **Short-term causes: current:** E, G, J; **Medium-term causes: recent:** A, D; **Long-term causes; historic:** B, C, F, H, I.

2. A = e;   B = d;   C = c;   D = b;   E = a

Page 24

3. a **True:** A, E, F; **False:** B, C, D, G

   b **B:** The trial began in February 1924 and the verdicts were given on 1 April 1924.

   C: There was a huge amount of public attention for the trial, both in Germany and in other countries.

   D: Hitler was treated with a lot of tolerance in court and allowed to make long speeches, cross-examine witnesses himself and interrupt other speakers. (Hitler's friend was the Minister for Justice in Bavaria, who arranged for Hitler's favourable treatment.)

   G: There was widespread disgust and amazement at the verdicts, even among right-wing groups. The light sentences given to Hitler, considering that his actions had led to four policemen being killed (as well as the theft of large sums of money, hostage-taking and destruction), caused a scandal.

4. a *Mein Kampf* put together Hitler's political views in one place, which made them easier for Germans to read and understand. *Mein Kampf* became central to the ideology of the Nazi Party.

   b Hitler's trial received widespread public attention. He realised he could use it to spread his ideas and make himself better known in Germany. Although the Nazi Party went through lean years between 1924 and 1928, it meant that Hitler was already well known when right-wing parties started to take advantage of the suffering caused by the Great Depression in 1929.

   c Hitler's decision that force was not a reliable route to power meant he decided the Nazi Party would win power through the democratic system, even though he hated democracy. This entailed changes in the Nazi Party to make it more electable.

Page 25

1. For example: Hitler did not smoke or drink; It was clear that Hitler was going to try to build up the popularity of his political party; Hitler had decided not to use violent methods in the future; Hitler deserved to be released early from prison because of his good behaviour.

2. The source content you use may be different from the example below, but what is important is the strength of the link between the student's inference and the enquiry.

   a Source B is useful for an enquiry into Hitler's change of approach for the Nazi Party after the Munich Putsch.

   b because it says/shows that Hitler had decided not to use violent methods in the future.

(c) This is useful because it suggests that Hitler realised that using force to take power in Germany was not going to work.

(3) **(a)** Source C is useful for an enquiry into reactions to Hitler's trial in 1924.

(b) because it shows that the defendants (those on trial), who had been military leaders, were allowed to appear in court in their military uniforms and carry swords.

(c) This is useful because it suggests that public perceptions would have been influenced by seeing these men as war heroes and upper class, respectable people. This would help them argue that they had acted for noble, serious reasons.

Page 26

(1) **(a)** Authoritativeness is the strongest criterion because of the origin of the book: Lurker was a prison warder with inside knowledge and experience.

(b) Objectivity is not very strong for Source B because the source's origin suggests this is someone who sympathised with Hitler's politics rather than being objective. This affects source reliability. Typicality is also weak, because this source does not provide an overview of opinion but is one person's view.

(2) For example:

Book published in 1933:

Useful because: this information might not otherwise have been recorded (typicality). Less useful: published in 1933 so 10 years after the event: recollections could be affected by hindsight (reliability).

Prison warder/later SS member:

Useful because: Lurker was an eyewitness to Hitler's imprisonment (authoritative). Less useful: Lurker went on to join the SS this suggests right-wing sympathies that might affect his objectivity (and reliability).

(3) **(a)** Origin.

(b) They can report on something they actually saw or experienced rather than reporting something second-hand.

(c) A limitation could be nature: the book was published 10 years after Hitler was sent to prison and this could mean Lurker's recollection is affected by hindsight, so is less reliable.

Page 27

(1) A and C

(2) The police report was written to convince the authorities and would have been based on evidence about Hitler from different police sources: reliability.

(3) The police wanted to keep Hitler in prison because they were concerned he would cause problems for the police again. This could make the police biased against Hitler, reducing objectivity.

(4) For example: Source C is useful to the enquiry because it warns that Hitler will 'without doubt' try to use force against the government again if he is released from prison. The source is from 1924, written by people directly involved in security in Bavaria, which makes it authoritative. Although the Bavarian police might have been biased against Hitler because of what happened in the Munich Putsch, in my view this source is very useful to the enquiry as it tells us that the police did not believe that Hitler had given up violence and they opposed his early release.

Page 28

(1) **Underline:** Because Source B is from a court trial, we know it would have been recorded accurately by someone in the court. [Source C] is a contemporary photo that helps us to see how Hitler, Ludendorff and others were represented in the media.

(2) **Circle:** the photo has been carefully posed to give this effect, so it is not an objective representation.

(3) **Double underline:** We know it would have been recorded accurately by someone in the court. That makes it more useful as we can be confident that Hitler really said this.

(4) **Not enough:** there is evaluation of one strength for Source B and one limitation of usefulness for Source C. The answer would be more secure if there were a couple of evaluations of usefulness for each source.

(5) No.

(6) **What is good:** the student selects valid content from the sources which could both be useful to the enquiry; the student uses nature and purpose to evaluate the content of both sources. The student also shows some knowledge of the period (see next unit) to consider the usefulness of the sources.

How the answer could be improved: by offering another evaluation of each source and then use these evaluations of the sources' strengths and limitations to make a judgement on 'how useful'.

Page 29

(1) Student's own response.

Unit 4
Page 32

(1) The enquiry is about the impact of unemployment in the years 1929–33.

(2) **Nature:** one strength could be that a graph is useful for an enquiry into the impact of unemployment because it allows you to compare unemployment from year to year.

Origin: the origin of the graph is useful because it is a trusted source of information = reliable data.

Purpose: the purpose of the graph is to provide information, perhaps for investors, on industry in Germany, which means it would need to be reliable data.

Page 33

(1) **Students should add in this order:** Wall Street Crash; share prices; 24 October 1929; major investors; ran out of money; German industries and farms; loans they depended on; cut back on their spending; numbers of unemployed.

Page 34

(2) B, C, F

(3)

General elections, 1929–32: seats in the Reichstag			
Political parties	May 1928	September 1930	July 1932
Social Democrats (SPD)	152	143	133
Nazi Party (NSDAP)	12	107	230
Communist Party (KPD)	54	77	89

(4) **True:** B, C; **False:** A, D

Page 35

1 **a** The first part of the answer is the inference: 'Source B suggests that workers were attracted to the KPD because while they could not afford to buy anything, factory owners stayed rich'.

b The inference is supported by the student's own knowledge: 'It is true that even those who still had jobs in 1932 faced falling income because employers tried to save money by cutting wages.'

2 For example: economic crisis; resentment of Weimar leaders for failure to solve problems; resentment of democracy: coalition governments not strong enough to solve problems; resentment of specific policies, e.g. Brüning's tax policies; appeal of Communists: ending exploitation of workers

3 For example: Source B suggests that people were facing 'unbelievable misery' because of the economic crisis and unemployment. Living standards did drop dramatically and this left people desperate for radical solutions, which helps to explain the rise in support for extremist parties.

Page 36

1 **a, b, c**

Source B says that the workers 'cannot afford to buy anything'. This would be useful for the enquiry because it would suggest that one reason for increasing support for extremist parties like the KPD was that workers were desperate because they could not afford to live. One problem with the source is that the author was a member of the Communist Party, which could affect its objectivity about the appeal of socialism, but it is true that wages were cut so that in 1932 they were 30% lower than in 1928, supporting the claim that even people in work could become desperate. That suggests that Source B makes a useful contribution to the enquiry.

b The student uses provenance (origin) to identify a limitation of the source content.

c The student uses their own historical knowledge to support a strength of the source content.

d Yes

2 C

3 **a** A   **b** B   **c** D

Page 37

1, 2 Source B = i (S), v (S), vi (W). Source C = ii (S), iii (S), iv (S)

3 For example: Source B suggests that thousands of the Nazis' political opponents were put into concentration camps in 1933 and tortured. The purpose of Source B was to shock readers and influence their opinion, which limits its reliability [weakness]. It is true that 4,000 Communists were arrested in March 1933 [strength], so it is certainly possible that thousands were arrested in Berlin. Sources written by opponents of the Nazis are not typical because it was so dangerous to speak out against the Nazi regime [strength].

Source C suggests that Germans approved of putting Communists and Social Democrats into concentration camps for re-education. Private letters to friends in 1933 should express the writer's real feelings, so Source C's nature strengthens its usefulness [strength], and Nazi propaganda also stressed that concentration camps were to re-educate political prisoners to stop them being a threat to the German community [strength], so it is useful to see how this propaganda had an effect on some Germans. The Nazis received 92% of the vote in the November 1933 election [strength], which suggests that (even if there was massive vote-rigging) a lot of Germans did not object to the removal of Communists and Social Democrats.

Page 38

1 The Nazis used fear of a Communist uprising following the Reichstag Fire (February 1933) to increase their popularity. This included arresting KPD supporters and Social Democrats. Source C is useful in helping explain why many Germans supported this, even though people were arrested and imprisoned without trial – many Germans were frightened of Communists and wanted a strong government to 'clean up' Germany. Because Source C is from private letters it is probably reliable at setting out how the author really felt about the use of concentration camps.

Source B is about opposition to the use of concentration camps. It suggests that the SA were very brutal and even murderous in the way they treated KPD and SPD prisoners. This is useful because at the time the Nazi government said that prisoners were not mistreated. They even allowed journalists to visit some concentration camps to show this. Source B was designed to convince people about 'Hitler's Crimes', which could affect its reliability as a source. However, it was dangerous to express negative opinions about the Nazis, which makes sources such as Source B very rare. That makes Source B very useful for this enquiry.

Both sources are therefore useful to the enquiry. In my view Source B is the most useful, because it is so rare to have sources from groups opposing the Nazi regime.

2 Judgements about usefulness are limited to one sentence at the end = lower level. Provenance is used to evaluate usefulness, and contextual knowledge is used to evaluate the strength of NOP = higher level. Contextual knowledge is used to evaluate content = higher level.

Page 39

1 Student's own response.

Unit 5

Page 42

1 D

2 The main difference between the two views is that View C advises students what they need to do to do well in this exam question, while View D gives a warning to students about spending too much time answering this question.

Page 43

1 A = d; B = a; C = e; D = b; E = c

2 **Cross out:** Roma; made it illegal to be gay; 1939; **Correction 1:** Roma should be changed to Slavs; **Correction 2:** The Nazis strengthened existing laws against homosexuality; **Correction 3:** 1933, not 1939.

Page 44

3 **Chronological order:** 1 = A; 2 = B; 3 = E; 4 = F; 5 = H; 6 = G; 7 = C; 8 = D

4 **a**, **d** and **a** are true. **b** the Olympic Games were in 1936; **c** Nazi leaders were given these instructions but not openly; **f** around 100 Jewish people were killed; **g** Jews were not allowed to claim for the damage on their insurance policies.)

5 Students should add in this order: 1935; Nuremberg; two laws; blood; citizens 'subjects'; right to vote; marrying; divorce.

Page 45

(1) Because/While; frequently/rarely; praised/criticised; clear/never clear; not supported/supported

(2) **(a)** Key 'opinion' words for Interpretation 1 could be: Now, hindsight, step-by-step path, total annihilation, not clear at the time.

Key 'opinion' words for Interpretation 2 could be: Hitler's purpose, plain and unchanging, meant to, carry out, extermination of the Jewish race.

(b) 'total annihilation' and 'extermination of the Jewish race' are both important but they do not point to differences between the interpretations: they both agree.

A good choice would be 'not clear at the time' and 'plain and unchanging' because this points to a difference between the two interpretations.

(c) Summary of Interpretation 1: It was not clear at the time that there was a step-by-step plan for the total annihilation of the Jews.

Summary of Interpretation 2: Hitler's plan to exterminate the Jews was plain and unchanging.

Page 46

(1) For example: **Underline:** Hitler's purpose; plain and unchanging; meant to carry out; German state should actually do; succeded; cold-blooded purpose

(2) Hitler's purpose was plain and unchanging/cold-blooded purpose; Extermination something the German state should actually do; Hitler's purpose was plain and unchanging

(3) The main difference is that Interpretation 1 says it was not clear at the time that Nazi persecution was leading to the extermination of the Jews, while Interpretation 2 says it was always clear that Hitler meant to exterminate the Jews.

Page 47

(1) **(a)** The second sentence should be double underlined as supporting detail.

(b) The two phrases in quotation marks are key 'opinion' terms for Skills boost 2.

(2) **(a)** For example: **What is important to keep in the answer:** A main difference between the interpretations is Interpretation 1 says it was not clear at the time that Nazi persecution was leading to the extermination of the Jews, while Interpretation 2 says it was always clear that Hitler meant to exterminate the Jews. For example, Interpretation 1 says a 'step-by-step path to annihilation… was not clear at the time'.

(b) The supporting detail needs to be for Interpretation 2's view and kept concise, e.g. Interpretation 2 says 'Hitler's purpose was plain and unchanging'.

Page 48

(1) A has not identified the main difference. B has identified the main difference: the whole answer could be circled.

(2) A has added supporting detail in the second sentence. B has not provided support for the key difference of view.

(3) Both answers are about as good as each other. A has good supporting detail but has not identified the main difference. B has identified the main difference but has not provided any supporting information from the interpretations.

(4) Student's own response. A sample answer is provided on page 47 (after the required cuts were made).

Page 49

(1) Student's own response.

Unit 6

Page 52

(1) Source B is a graph of the number of unemployed people in Germany between 1933 and 1939. It shows that unemployment declined between 1933 and 1939, from 6 million to 100,000.

Source C is a description of the daily routine at a labour service camp, giving the times at which different activities were scheduled and showing that the day was very busy.

(2) C and D

Page 53

(1) Missing answers could include: the armed forces, rearmament, prisons.

Sample descriptions: **The Labour Service:** By the mid-1930s, half a million unemployed people were in the Labour Service and no longer counted as unemployed.

The armed forces: 1.3 million men in the armed forces by 1939 who would have otherwise needed jobs.

Rearmament: This involved huge government orders of weapons, equipment and vehicles from German industry, creating thousands of jobs that would not otherwise have existed.

Women and Jews: Jews were forced out of their jobs; women were also forced out or expected to quit work. Neither group was then counted as unemployed.

Public works: The huge programme of public works (e.g. autobahns) in the 1930s created thousands of 'artificial' jobs; the government could not have afforded to keep spending on these much longer.

Prisons: hundreds of thousands of Germans who had previously had jobs were imprisoned in jails or concentration camps.

Page 54

(2) A, B, D, E and F are true; C and G are false.

(3) A = c; B = a; C = b

(4) For example:

The Labour Front: a way it improved standards of living: made sure employers did not decrease pay below a minimum, or increase working hours. Limitation: workers no longer had the right to negotiate with employers themselves/go on strike; the DAF increased the maximum length of the working week (by about 6 hours), the DAF also could punish workers accused of disrupting production.

Strength through Joy: a way it improved standards of living: made trips and holidays much more affordable for huge numbers of poorer Germans, made the goal of having a family car seem affordable for most Germans. Limitation: the best trips were usually reserved for the most loyal workers; the Volkswagen saving scheme never delivered any cars because production switched to military requirements with the war.

Beauty of Labour: a way it improved standards of living: nearly 34,000 companies are thought to have improved facilities for their workers (according to Nazi statistics). Limitation: workers were usually expected to make the improvements themselves, without any extra pay.

Page 55

1

	Interpretation 1's view	Interpretation 2's view	Source B's message	Source C's message
Nazi policies to reduce unemployment	Nazi policies overall reduced unemployment from 6 million to 1 million, were popular	Nazi policies included RAD, which gave men work but were not popular – as being in RAD was too like being in the army.	Provides reliable evidence of huge reduction by 1939	Provides evidence of military-style regime in labour service camp (like RAD)

2 Interpretation 1 is supported by Source B and Interpretation 2 is supported by Source C.

3 For example: evidence; Source B; unemployment policies; work in a labour camp; Source C; military lines

Page 56

1 C and F

2 For example: One reason for their different views is that they focus on different things about unemployment policies. While Interpretation 1 has a wider emphasis on how Hitler's different economic policies for economic recovery successfully reduced unemployment, Interpretation 2 has a narrower emphasis: on the RAD and its popularity.

3 For example: One reason for their different views is that the interpretations focus on different things about Nazi unemployment policies. While Interpretation 1 has a wide emphasis on the Nazis' policies for economic recovery, Interpretation 2 is focused on one policy only. For example, Interpretation 1 says it was a range of economic policies that 'successfully achieved a fall in unemployment' over the period 1933–39, while Interpretation 2 only considers the RAD and how those who worked for the RAD felt about it.

4 Student's own response. (The suggested answer to question 3 above is fairly concise.)

Page 57

1 **a** Extract C **b** Extract A **c** Extract B is explaining a difference based on historians' emphasis.

2 A

Page 58

1 A: Evidence from the period.

2 For example: **Cross out:** for the different views; evidence like; and keep them out of the 'people's community' until 're-education' meant they were no longer a threat.; concentration camps and other elements; evidence like

Page 59

1 For example: **Historians' emphasis:** the interpretations emphasise different aspects of the Nazi police state: Interpretation 2 introduces the different components of the police state as an overview, while Interpretation 1 focuses on the question of whether people supported the police state out of fear or because they agreed with the regime's aims.

Historical context: the interpretations do not actually contradict each other. The Nazis were aiming to encourage support from people who were worried about Communism, for example, as well as to frighten those who might otherwise have spoken out against the regime or opposed it. Interpretation 1 sees more people supporting the Nazis' police state than terrified by it, while Interpretation 2 is interested in the impact of the police state on those people who weren't convinced by indoctrination.

2 Student's own response.

Unit 7

Page 62

1 A: The whole diagram: the analysis points drive all aspects of the answer.

B: Write your answer, remembering to explain and justify your conclusion.

C: Use your contextual knowledge to evaluate the points supporting Interpretation X/Do the same to evaluate the points supporting Interpretation Y's counter-argument/ Analyse Interpretation Y to identify the points and evidence that counter the view in X/Add in any key points missing from the interpretations

D: Your plan must be organised to review the two views

2 A is correct and B is not; C is correct and D is not; E is incorrect and F is true.

Page 63

1 A = c; B = b; C = d; D = e; E = a

2 B

Page 64

3 **March 1932:** Presidential elections: Hitler wins 11 million votes; **April 1932:** Presidential elections: Hitler wins 13 million votes; **May 1932:** Von Papen becomes Chancellor; **July 1932:** Reichstag elections: Nazis win 230 seats; **December 1932:** Von Schleicher becomes Chancellor; **January 1933:** Hitler becomes Chancellor

4 Students should add in this order: aeroplane; Communist; Hindenburg; Papen; July; 230; Chancellor; rejected; Schleicher; army; Hindenburg; Papen; pocket.

Page 65

1 For example:

Points from Interpretation 2	Evidence used?	What emphasis?
Weimar Germany already had serious problems before the 1929 economic crisis	Contrasts stable societies with Weimar Germany, which already had a 'political and social crisis'	Sees democratic Weimar Germany as having no chance of surviving because it was already so unstable

Page 66

1 + **2** The + ~ – scores are just for illustration: as long as they can be explained, there are no wrong judgements.

Points from Interpretation 1	Contextual knowledge that supports the point	Contextual knowledge that challenges the point	+ ~ −
Germany needed a strong leader/ people saw Hitler in a religious way	Hitler's speeches were carefully rehearsed to deliver a powerful message and a powerful emotional impact	Hitler's image was damaged by the street violence of the SA. In July 1932, around 100 were killed in fighting between the SA and KPD.	+
Hitler appealed to many different social groups and both genders	In the 1930 elections, the Nazis got 60% of the vote in some rural areas 43% of new Nazi Party members were under 30	Although the Nazi Party targeted workers with slogans like 'Work and Bread', more workers preferred the KPD	~
Hitler's speeches and Nazi propaganda were reasons for the growth in support	Hitler used an aeroplane in election campaigns in 1930 and 1932	The Nazi vote fell in November 1932, to 196 seats, despite strong speeches and propaganda	−

Page 67

(1) **a, b** The + ~ − scores are just for illustration: as long as they can be explained, there are no wrong judgements.

Points from Interpretation 2	Contextual knowledge that supports the point	Contextual knowledge that challenges the point	+ ~ −
Weimar Germany already had serious problems before the 1929 economic crisis	Reparation payments were still at £50 million a year in 1930. The German economy depended on US loans	Unemployment fell to 1.3 million by 1928; real wages rose by 25% from 1925 to 1928	−
People blamed the Republican leaders for the crisis/for not being able to deal with it	SPD votes dropped: in 1928 the SPD had 152 seats, in 1932 this fell to 133	The Nazi vote fell in November 1932, to 196 seats, despite the crisis continuing	~

(2) A

Page 68

(1) **a, b** and **c**

… Interpretation 1 sees support for the Nazis being because Germans saw Hitler as their 'saviour and redeemer'. Sources from the period often refer to Hitler's charisma and appeal, and there is no doubt that many Germans did see him as like a religious 'saviour'. Interpretation 1 also carefully selects other ways in which Nazi propaganda 'captured the imagination of the masses', and strongly implies that propaganda was

significant in creating an inspiring illusion of Germany's future that convinced 'the masses' to support the Nazis. However, in my view propaganda and Hitler's personal appeal alone cannot explain the rise in support for the Nazis after 1930 (100,000 people joined the party between September and December of 1930). The Nazis' message was based on Mein Kampf which was published five years earlier, and Hitler's speeches had been powerful emotional performances since at least 1923 (for example, his speeches at his trial). Therefore I do not agree with Interpretation 1's emphasis on Hitler's appeal and Nazi propaganda: other factors must have been important in explaining the rapid growth in support for the Nazis after 1929.

(2) I agree with Interpretation 2 that the main reason for the growth in support for the Nazis was the economic crisis following the Wall Street Crash in 1929. Interpretation 2's opinion is that when an economic crisis hits, people inevitably blame their own government. People were desperate for a way out of the crisis, and saw the Weimar government as unable to help. This allowed opponents of democratic government to exploit this resentment, as Interpretation 2 states. Evidence for this includes the fall in votes for SPD: 152 seats in 1928 but 133 in 1932, while the Nazi Party increased their share of the vote from 18% in 1930 to 38% in 1932. Interpretation 2 makes the point that the crisis was 'bound to' cause serious problems in Weimar Germany. I agree that Weimar Germany was very fragile – its economy depended on US loans – but rapid growth in support for the Nazis did not happen before 1929 because before then unemployment was falling (down to 1.3 million in 1928) and wages were rising (up 25% between 1925 and 1928). Therefore I agree that it was the economic situation that allowed Nazi propaganda to have a mass effect. As Interpretation 2 argues, the 'situation made it possible.'

Page 69

(1) Student's own response.

Unit 8

Page 72

(1) D, B, C, A

(2) I agree more with Interpretation 1 than Interpretation 2 about how effective Nazi policies were at encouraging youth loyalty. Interpretation 1 is more convincing about most young people going along with Nazi youth organisations, rather than resisting them: even if they did dislike the Hitler Youth lessons and military drill, they did like being together as a group, being able to do sport activities and being protected from having to do everything parents and teachers said. Although Edelweiss Pirate groups were set up by young people who really hated the 'conformity and politicised tone' of Nazi Youth groups, there were only around 2,000 Edelweiss Pirates by 1939, compared with 8 million Hitler Youth members. Not all these Hitler Youth members were loyal to the Nazi Party: most probably would rather not have had to go, but I agree with Interpretation 1 that the Nazis were effective in making organisations like the Hitler Youth something that young people took for granted rather than something they thought about resisting.

Page 73

(1) B, C, F and G

(2) A + e; B + d; C + a; D + b; E + c

Page 74

(3) political; Nazi Party; oath; courses; lessons; Jews; report; parents

(4) a The Nazi Teachers League

  b Lessons started and finished by students saying 'Heil Hitler'; classrooms were decorated with Nazi flags and posters.

(5) For example: some young people did not join the Hitler Youth because they objected to the Nazis' aims of making all young people into Nazi believers; the authorities were worried about young people who were in the Hitler Youth being influenced against the organisation by outsiders.

Page 75

(1) Generally agree.

(2) For example: The student generally agrees with Interpretation 1's view that most young people just took the Hitler Youth for granted, mainly because there were not really any alternatives. However, the student was concerned that Interpretation 1 did not recognise that by the end of the 1930s most young people were reluctant to attend Nazi youth organisations and attendance had to be made compulsory.

Page 76

(1) a **Tick:** A, D, G and H; **Cross:** B, C, E and F

  b D, A, G, H is probably the most effective order, although H could come earlier, e.g. D, H, A, G

(2) A; G; G: G; G; D; H

Page 77

(1) a Interpretation 1: ++/generally agree

  Interpretation 2: −−/generally disagree

  b **Interpretation 1:** Argument from interpretation: because there were not really any alternatives for young people. Evidence from own knowledge: because other young groups were closed down in 1933.

  Interpretation 2: Argument from interpretation: many German teenagers rejected the Hitler Youth Evidence from own knowledge: 'many' isn't true because there were so few Edelweiss Pirates compared with millions of Hitler Youth.

(2) For example: I strongly disagree with Interpretation 2's view that many German teenagers rejected the Hitler Youth, meaning that Nazi policies to encourage youth loyalty would have failed. My main reason for this is that there were so few Edelweiss Pirates (2,000) compared with millions of Hitler Youth, which does not support Interpretation 2's claim about 'many'.

I find Interpretation 1's view generally more convincing because there really were no alternatives to Nazi youth organisations for young people after the Church youth groups were shut down in 1933, so most young people would have gone along with the Nazi youth organisations and accepted them as part of their lives.

In conclusion, Nazi policies to encourage youth loyalty were generally unsuccessful, but they did succeed in making young people go along with the Nazi organisations without really thinking about it.

Page 78

(1) C

(2) I strongly agree with Interpretation 2's view that Nazi policies to encourage youth loyalty failed. Interpretation 2 uses the Edelweiss Pirates as evidence of the way many German teenagers completely rejected Nazi youth organisations, especially the constant political pressure on Hitler Youth members to swear loyalty to the Nazis and to learn to think and act in Nazi ways. One criticism of Interpretation 2 is that there were only ever small numbers of Edelweiss Pirates, 2000 in total, but there are good reasons to think that many more German teens were very reluctant to go to Nazi youth organisations. In 1938 attendance had to be made compulsory, because only 25% of young people were attending Nazi youth organisations. This is also why I only partly agree with Interpretation 1, which argues that young people went along with Nazi youth organisations because they didn't know anything different. While I agree that many teens would have enjoyed the leisure activities, I am convinced that the low attendance figures prove that Nazi policies to encourage youth loyalty were why the youth organisations became unpopular, showing that the policy failed.

Key: Overall judgement Link to question focus

Page 79

(1) Student's own response.